Anonymous

Report on a Series of Red-Hot Furnace Crown Experiments

to ascertain the result of injecting the feed-water into a boiler when short

of water and with fires burning

Anonymous

Report on a Series of Red-Hot Furnace Crown Experiments
to ascertain the result of injecting the feed-water into a boiler when short of water and with fires burning

ISBN/EAN: 9783337269807

Printed in Europe, USA, Canada, Australia, Japan

Cover: Foto ©Andreas Hilbeck / pixelio.de

More available books at **www.hansebooks.com**

NCHESTER STEAM USERS' ASSOCIATION.

REPORT

ON A SERIES

URNACE CRO

NTS,

THE RESULT OF

ED-

TO A BOILER WH

AND WITH FIRES

MANCHESTER :
CHAS. SEVER, PRINTER. LITHOGRAPHER, &c., LONG MILLGATE.
1889.

THE M

STEAM USE   T,

PREVENTION OF S

ATTAINMENT OF ECONO   EAM.

ESTA

9, MOUNT STREET, A   R.

GUARAN

HENRY

JOHN RAMSBOTT

EX

CHARLES HEATON, Esq., Bol   urn.
THOMAS SCHOFIELD, Esq., Ma   dleton.
SAMUEL RIGBY, Esq., Chester   alifax.
   Armitage and Rigbys, Warring   hester.
JAMES TAYLOR, Esq., Cire   alford.
   Gloucester (late of Thomas   orton.
   and Bro., Wigan).

THE MANCHES

CH

LAVINGT

CHIEF ENGINEER'S REPORT

ON A SERIES OF

RED-HOT FURNACE CROWN EXPERIMENTS.

To the Members of the Executive Committee of the Manchester Steam Users' Association.

GENTLEMEN,

I now beg to present to you my report on the series of Red-Hot Furnace Crown experiments I have conducted, with the assistance of several members of the M.S.U.A. engineering staff, in accordance with your instructions, in order to throw light on the vexed question of the effect of injecting feed water into a boiler when short of water and with the furnace-crowns red-hot. This report has been unavoidably deferred on account of the difficulty of conducting such an enterprise and the numerous interruptions of the regular work of the Association.

VIEWS VERY GENERALLY ENTERTAINED WITH REGARD TO THE EFFECT OF SHOWERING WATER ON TO RED-HOT FURNACE CROWNS.

The idea that nearly every explosion is attributable to shortness of water has been very generally entertained for a considerable number of years, and has had a very mischievous tendency.

It is true that some explosions arise from this cause. If the furnace crowns are rendered red-hot, the plates become so weakened thereby that they may rend at the ordinary working pressure of steam. Such was the case in an explosion which occurred at Bilston on Wednesday, November 5th, 1884, when three boilers of the plain cylindrical egg-ended externally-fired type blew up together, the fragments being widely scattered. Many other cases might be cited. The investigations of the Association, however, show that explosions from shortness of water form but a small proportion of the total number, and that they do not exceed more than one in six. Further, that when they arise from internally-fired boilers, they are not, as a rule, very destructive. The furnace crown is rent, but the shell remains uninjured, and the boiler is not stirred from its seat; so that unless some-one is standing directly in front of the furnace, and thus in line with the torrent of steam and hot water that rushes out of the furnace mouth, such explosions do not result in personal injury. This may be accepted as a general rule, though exceptions in individual cases will be found, as for instance when the space is confined, as on board ship, in illustration of which the explosion on H.M.s.s. "Thistle" may be referred to, which occurred on Wednesday, November 3rd, 1869, when as many as 11 persons were killed. These deaths resulted from scalding. There were no fragments nor flying *débris*. The shell was not rent, but remained intact, and the boiler was not stirred from its seat. Such is the general behaviour of the boiler, when of the internally-fired class, on the occurrence of an explosion from shortness of water.

Many explosions, however, in which the shells have been violently torn in pieces and the fragments scattered to great distances, have been attributed, without foundation, to shortness of water. It has been thought that if the furnace crown of a boiler were laid bare and allowed to become red-hot, and then the feed turned on, so large an amount of steam would be instantaneously generated that the safety-valves would be unable to carry it off, and the increase of pressure would be so sudden, and so great, that the shell would be burst open and the boiler blown to pieces.

This view appears to have been held in the early days of steam by high authorities, and it may be of interest to quote some of the statements made by them on this subject.

In the year 1839 Captain Pringle, R.E., and Mr. Josiah Parkes, M. Inst. C.E., were appointed by the Lords of the Committee of Privy Council for Trade to undertake an inquiry into "the causes of "steam-boat accidents and the best means of preventing their recur- "rence," and in their report the Commissioners treat on the subject of steam boiler explosions at considerable length, referring to one of a very violent and disastrous character that occurred at Hull, on board the steam-ship "Union," on the 7th of June, 1837, killing 24 persons.

It appears from the report that the boiler in this case was of the rectangular description, "with the top slightly arched and supported "inside by 60 stays of 1½ or 2 inches square wrought-iron bars." When the boiler burst the top was completely rent from the bottom, and all the stays broken. The top, weighing about 3 tons, was thrown to a distance of 30 or 40 yards. "One of the men who stood on the "deck of the vessel above the boiler was thrown about 50 feet high, "and fell on the top of a house from 60 to 80 yards from the vessel. "Other persons were thrown to considerable distances. Bales of goods, "casks, bags of flour, and other heavy articles, were carried still further, "while the vessel was shattered below the water mark and sunk."

Referring to this explosion, the Commissioners state:—"It is "attributed with great apparent reason to the *instantaneous disengage-* "*ment of an immense volume of steam* produced by the oscillation or "listing of the vessel, the boiler, a rectangular one, being at the time "short of water, and the upper plates of the furnace on the higher "side of the vessel being probably red-hot, or nearly so. *No ordinary* "*number of safety-valves could have liberated the amount of steam* "*generated.*"

The Commissioners in conducting their investigation issued a list of inquiries to engineers, shipbuilders, and others, and in the replies received from several of these parties allusion was made to the boiler explosion on board the steamship "Union" just referred to.

Mr. John Thorney, Coroner, Hull, referring to the inquest which had been held in consequence of the explosion, states that the opinions of scientific men with regard thereto were very unsettled, some holding "that highly-heated steam rapidly generated was sufficient to occasion "all the terrific violence in the case of the explosion under con- "sideration, while others held it was occasioned by the ignition of "hydrogen gas, produced by the decomposition of the water on "coming in contact with the red-hot furnaces." Mr. Thorney goes on to say, "basing my conclusions on the evidence given at the inquest, "I am of opinion that, owing to the engineer of the steamship "'Union,' either being deceived by the water-gauge taps of the "boiler or from his inattention to the quantity of water in the boiler, "the tops of the furnaces were bare of water and became heated to a "red-heat; that the steam in the boiler, from the imperfect action of "the safety-valve, had not free and proper escape; that such steam "coming in contact with the red-hot furnaces would become highly "heated, and thereby *greatly increased in expansive force*; that while "the boiler was in this state the vessel had oscillated, from the "persons on board moving from side to side, and from goods being "carried across her to the adjoining steamboat, and that the water "between the furnaces—which are supposed to have been red-hot at "the top surface—was by such oscillation thrown over the top of "such furnaces, *whereby a great volume of highly-elastic steam would* "*be instantly generated,* and which, having no sufficient outlet to "escape, caused the fearful catastrophe."

The well known engineer, the late Mr. John Scott Russell, C.E., builder of the steamship "Great Eastern," stated:—"If the water in a boiler "gets too low, the furnaces are uncovered and become red-hot, and "thus when the time of starting occurs, the motion of the vessel and "the action of the pump raise the water on to the red-hot metal, and

"*steam is generated so rapidly that an explosion almost inevitably ensues.*
"This is exactly what took place in the case of the explosion that
"occurred on board the steamship 'Union' at Hull."

The celebrated engineers, Messrs. Maudsley and Field, of Lambeth,
London, endorsed this view.

Mr. James Oldham, C. E., Hull, took the same view of the cause
of the explosion as the other engineers referred to above, stating
that he "had no doubt the furnaces had been red-hot, and on their
"becoming again covered with water there would be *instantaneously*
"*created a powerful, uncontrollable, and highly elastic vapour*, which
"was the immediate cause of the catastrophe, and which *no boiler*
"*would be strong enough to resist.*"

Very similar opinions were entertained at that time by other
scientific men.

On the 30th of March, 1841, Mr. Charles Schafhaeutl, M.D., Assoc.
Inst. C.E , read a paper before the Institution of Civil Engineers on
"The circumstances under which explosions frequently occur in steam
"boilers, and the causes to which such explosions may be assigned."

In this paper the writer discredits the view that boilers burst from
a gradual accumulation of steam pressure, but considers that they
burst from the sudden generation of some explosive force. He says--
"Of the explosions which occur in steam boilers, it may with reason
"be assumed that a very large proportion must be assigned to some
"*other cause than the simple pressure of the steam* due to the
"accumulation of a surplus quantity in the boiler or to the over-
"loading of the safety valve, since many cases of explosions
"have occurred in which it has been ascertained beyond all doubt
"that the safety valve was in perfect order, and also cases in which it
"had acted immediately before the explosion, or was even in action at
"the instant of that occurrence. Undoubted and indisputable facts of
"this nature, and the considerations hereafter referred to, show that
"these calamitous occurrences must be referred to *other causes than*
"*the gradual increase of pressure in the steam*, or defects in the ordinary
"safety valve." Dr. Schafhaeutl goes on to suggest that explosions
are due "to a force *momentary in its nature*, tearing asunder the
"plates of the boiler at the instant of its generation, and before there
"is time for its transmission to the safety valve. The existence of
"a force of this nature, *sudden in its origin and instantaneous in its*
"*duration*, has suggested itself to many minds."

In the course of the discussion that ensued on Dr. Schafhaeutl's
paper, Mr. Parkes, M. Inst. C. E., stated "he had been occupied
"for several years in collecting facts illustrative of the phenomena of

" steam boiler explosions." His opinion was that " though the simple
" elastic force of the steam might *occasionally* account for the rending
" of a boiler, that cause was *insufficient* to explain many well known
" phenomena, such as the projection of an entire boiler from its seat,
" the separation of a boiler into two parts, the one remaining quiescent,
" the other being driven to a great distance, &c. He was of opinion
" that *a very sudden development of force* could alone have produced
" such effects. .   .   .   .   and that a " force *different*
" *from, and greater than*, the simple pressure of the steam was
" the principal agent." He considered that so sudden a generation
of steam would take place from " a thin sheet or wave of water "
passing over a red-hot furnace crown that " *no number of safety-valves*
" *could deprive the steam of its instantaneous force*, so as to save the
" boiler from destruction."

THE M.S.U.A. DISSENTS FROM THE VIEWS GENERALLY ENTERTAINED
WITH REGARD TO THE EFFECT OF SHOWERING WATER ON TO
RED-HOT FURNACE CROWNS.

The M.S.U.A. considers the views given above to be erroneous, and
though they may have been modified by the scientific men who first
enunciated them, and in all probability were so modified as experience
in the use of steam and in the investigation of steam boiler explosions
increased, yet they took deep root in the public mind, and have
continued to be generally entertained to the present day.

A few years since a very destructive explosion occurred at one of
Her Majesty's dockyards, the boiler being torn in pieces, the adjoining
one dislodged, and considerable damage done to surrounding property.
The cause was wasting of the plates in the outer shell by external
corrosion. They were eaten away till they were as thin as an old
sixpence. Yet evidence was given by three eminent scientific
witnesses at the Coroner's inquest to the effect that the explosion
arose from shortness of water, though the furnace crowns were not
rent, or even bulged out of shape. The shell was rent, and not the
furnace tubes. These witnesses assumed that the attendant had
neglected his duty, allowed the water supply in the boiler to run short,
and then suddenly re-admitted it, when they supposed *an excessive
and uncontrollable pressure of steam had been generated* which burst
the shell, and caused the explosion. In consequence of this evidence
the jury concluded that "the deaths of the deceased were caused by
" the accidental explosion of a boiler, and that such explosion resulted
" from an insufficient supply of water." Thus the onus of the explosion
was thrown on the engineman who had been killed. The verdict was

as unfair to the interests of science as it was to the poor engineman who lost his life by looking after a worn-out boiler.

Again, in a recent report issued by the Board of Trade, regarding an explosion which occurred from the bursting of a locomotive boiler on a public railway, the Board of Trade Inspector, who is a Major-General in the Royal Engineers, states, "After a careful consideration "of all the circumstances connected with this explosion, I am unable "to arrive at any other opinion than that it was caused by a *sudden* "*generation of very high pressure steam* acting with irresistible force "alike on the firebox and barrel of the boiler, and which force neither "the safety valves, nor the steam pipe which was presumably open— "as the train was in motion—were able to deal with. . . . . "Explosions of a nature somewhat similar to the present one, and to "be explained only by the fact of *a sudden generation of high pressure* "*steam*, have occurred before this."

A further illustration was recently afforded during the course of some legal proceedings arising out of an explosion which occurred at Garmouth, in Morayshire, Scotland, on the 4th of August, 1884, killing the fireman. From the Report of No. 88 Preliminary Inquiry under the Boiler Explosions Act, it appears that the explosion in question arose from the collapse of the internal firebox of a small vertical boiler, and was due to excessive pressure in consequence of the boiler not being equipped with any safety valve. The recklessness displayed in the working of the boiler was so great that the Procurator-Fiscal charged the owner of the boiler, as well as the manager of the works and the engineman, with culpable homicide, and the trial came off at Elgin on October 28th, 1884. The two engineers who had investigated the explosion on behalf of the Procurator-Fiscal, as well as the Board of Trade Surveyor who held the Preliminary Inquiry, agreed that the explosion was due simply to excessive pressure. The owner, however, in his defence, called several witnesses to prove that the explosion was the result of shortness of water, and could not be accounted for in any other way. One witness, who was an engineer, thought there had been "a sudden generation of steam which would act like gunpowder." A second witness, who said he was an engineer on the Great North of Scotland Railway, "formed the opinion that the boiler had been short "of water, and *cold water had been thrown in.*" A third witness, who stated he had been in the boiler-making trade for 21 years, "came to the conclusion that the water had got low, and on being "turned on again steam was generated so rapidly that an explosion "took place which would be *something the same as gunpowder.*" A fourth said that "if a boiler were short of water and the cold feed "were turned on an explosion would ensue, and *a safety-valve on* "*the boiler would not affect the matter one way or another.*" A fifth, who was an Inspector for a Boiler Insurance Company, said "the "uptake had been red-hot, and he attributed the explosion to the "*injection of cold water,*" adding that "from the appearance of the "boiler the explosion must have been caused by *a sudden generation* "*of steam.*" The result of the trial was that the jury returned a verdict of "Not guilty," thus practically endorsing the view advanced by the witnesses for the defence. The manner in which the boiler failed entirely contradicted this. Had the explosion been due to shortness of water, the crown plate would have been the part of the firebox to suffer most severely, as that would have been first laid bare, whereas the firebox did not give way at the crown but at the side, close to the bottom.[1]

THE M.S.U.A. CONSIDERS THE VIEWS GENERALLY ENTERTAINED WITH REGARD TO SHOWERING WATER ON TO RED-HOT FURNACE-CROWNS MOST MISCHIEVOUS.

The erroneous views quoted above come to the front on the occurrence of nearly every explosion. Their prevalence is mischievous. They divert attention from the true cause of explosions, which, in the great majority of cases, is either the original malconstruction of the boiler, or the dilapidated condition into which it has been allowed to fall.

Further, such views have had a mischievous effect with regard to the explosions of circulating boilers, in consequence of which they were for years attributed to the wrong cause. They were supposed to be due to the boiler being allowed to run dry during a frost and to the re-introduction of the feed on the occurrence of a thaw; whereas they are due simply to the gradual accumulation of pressure through the choking of the outlets. The remedy is to equip the boiler with a small reliable safety-valve, and no circulating boiler has been known to burst when so fitted. Sometimes circulating boiler explosions

---

NOTE.—[1]Many other cases illustrating the prevalence of the erroneous views regarding Shortness of Water have been recorded from time to time in the M.S.U.A. Reports. See Nos. 1, 6, 17, and 19 Explosions, December Report, 1878; No. 35 Explosion, December, 1877; No. 39 Explosion, September, 1873; No. 23 Explosion, November, 1867; No. 15 Explosion, June, 1867; No. 50 Explosion, 1866, see Report for June, 1868; No. 49 Explosion, November, 1866; No. 27 Explosion, October, 1866; No. 45 Explosion, September, 1866; Nos. 26 and 17 Explosions, July, 1866; No. 14 Explosion, April, 1866; No. 23 Explosion, 1865, see Report for January, 1866; No. 39 Explosion, December, 1865; Nos. 8 and 9 Explosions, August, 1865; No. 20 Explosion, May, 1865; No. 26 Explosion, 1864, see Reports for December, 1864, and August, 1865; No. 25 Explosion, December, 1864; No. 10 Explosion, May, 1864; see also Reports for December, 1862, and March, 1862. In 12 of these cases the attendant was killed by the explosion, while in two other cases he was wrongfully committed for trial on a charge of "manslaughter."

occur at a time of the year when there can be no frost. One such occurred at a mansion near Kenilworth on July 21st, 1886, killing one person and injuring another ; another at a mansion in Darlington on August 26th, 1869, injuring one person : and a third at a first-class hotel in London on October 19th, 1868, injuring six persons. In each case there were stop-taps in the circulating pipes, and in each case the taps were shut, while in no case was there any re-introduction of the feed.

The M.S.U.A. conducts Experiments on Injecting Water into Red-hot Circulating Boilers.

To throw light on this subject, the M.S.U.A., as long since as 1867, conducted some experiments to ascertain the result of injecting cold water into some circulating household boilers when red-hot, and found that no explosion resulted. An account of these experiments was given in the M.S.U.A. Report for February, 1867, and repeated in the Report for December, 1878.

Regarding the view to be erroneous, that an instantaneous and ungovernable amount of steam is generated by throwing a little water on to the red-hot furnace crowns of a boiler, it was thought that it might be well in the event of the water supply in a boiler running short to turn on the feed and thus to reduce the pressure of steam, cool down the furnaces, and arrest collapse. While past experiments clearly showed that no injury would occur to the shell from the adoption of this course, the question was raised : What would be the effect upon the furnace crowns ? It has been found unwise in cooling boilers to pour in cold water after blowing out the hot, as it tends to contract the plates at the bottom of the shell and put a heavy strain upon the ring seams of rivets, sometimes causing seam rips. It is also unwise to introduce the feed at a low level, as the ring seams of rivets at the bottom of the shell have been known to rip from this cause, through the severe contraction induced. It was, therefore, asked : If the feed be suddenly turned on when the furnaces are red-hot, might not the transverse seam rips that have been met with at the bottom of the shell, be produced in the furnace crowns ? And further, What might be the effect on the overheated furnace crowns generally ?

The question was submitted to several engineers of experience, but though they were fully aware that the specific heat of iron compared with water was so low that no large volume of steam would be generated, all hesitated to give an opinion as to what might be the behaviour of the furnace crowns under such treatment, and could suggest no other method of solving the problem than that of instituting a practical trial.

THE M.S.U.A. DECIDES TO INSTITUTE A SERIES OF EXPERIMENTS ON A FULL-SIZED LANCASHIRE BOILER TO ASCERTAIN THE EFFECT OF SHOWERING WATER ON TO RED-HOT FURNACE CROWNS.

On the matter being brought before the consideration of the Committee of the M.S.U.A., it was resolved to have the experiment tried on a practical scale, and that a full sized mill boiler should be laid down for the purpose.

On considering the mode of carrying out the experiments, it was at once apparent that they were not very easy of accomplishment. It was no simple task to deal with a full-sized boiler when under steam pressure, with the fires burning briskly, and the furnace crowns red-hot. Nor were there wanting advisers who enlarged upon the danger incurred, and predicted disaster. Precautions were taken, as will be seen in the following report, not merely for the protection of the observers, but also for the protection of persons outside the works, and, in deference to the opinions expressed on the subject, the pressure of steam in the boiler was lowered after the first two or three tests had been made. Having regard to the nature of the experiments and the prognostications that had been expressed, considerable satisfaction was felt when the series of trials was brought to a conclusion without injury to any one.

As is usual in conducting experimental investigations, in which the appliances are out of the common way and improvised for the occasion, many impediments were met with. These need only be hinted at and not entered on in detail. Suffice it to say that they tended to lengthen the period over which the trials extended ; added to which the pressure of the regular duties of the Association only allowed the experiments to be conducted as opportunity offered.

ARRANGEMENTS FOR EXPERIMENTS.

SELECTION OF SITE.—The first step to be taken was to select a site for the experiments. It was desirable to conduct them at or near to some engineering workshop for convenience in making the necessary preparations, but at the same time it was not desirable to conduct them in close proximity to a number of dwelling-houses. It was not easy to meet with a spot which precisely fulfilled these conditions ; but on the whole, a piece of open ground on the premises of the late Mr. Joseph Clayton, Preston, and adjoining his boiler shop, appeared the most suitable, and therefore Mr. Clayton was requested to allow the experiments to be conducted at his works, which he was good enough to consent to do.

DESCRIPTION OF THE BOILER AND FITTINGS.—The boiler selected was of the ordinary Lancashire type, with plain furnace tubes, lap-jointed and single-riveted, and not strengthened with flanged seams or encircling rings. It was thought this would give a fuller test than if a boiler of the modern and improved type of construction were adopted, in which the furnace tubes are welded at the longitudinal joints and strengthened circumferentially with flanged seams or other similar means.

The boiler measured 27 feet 9 inches in length, 7 feet in diameter in the shell, and 3 feet in the furnace tubes. The thickness of the plates was $\frac{7}{16}$ inch in the shell, $\frac{9}{16}$ inch in the ends, and $\frac{7}{16}$ inch in the furnace tubes. The material was iron throughout. The ends, both back and front, were strengthened with four gussets above the furnace tubes, while there were two at the front end and one at the back end below.

The fire-grates measured 6 feet in length by 3 feet in width, thus giving 18 square feet of grate surface in each furnace.

The boiler was set in the usual way on two longitudinal side walls, the flames, after leaving the internal flue tubes, passing under the boiler, and then, lastly, along the sides.

The following is a list of the fittings and mountings with which the boiler was equipped :—

Two feed-valves, $2\frac{1}{2}$ inches in diameter, both of them fixed to the front end of the boiler, one at the right-hand side, the other at the left, the centre of the inlet in each case being 6 inches above the level of the furnace crowns. To each of these valves was fixed inside the boiler a horizontal perforated feed dispersion pipe. As a rule, in ordinary practice these dispersion pipes are straight, and in the M.S.U.A. standard boiler they run along on one side, and within about 5 inches of the shell. Sometimes they are in three lengths of 5 feet each, the first two lengths, counting from the front end of the boiler, being blind, and the third perforated. In this case the dispersion pipe was in two lengths of 6 feet 6 inches each, the first length being blind, and the second perforated on one side with 38 holes set in a row. Although it is the ordinary practice to introduce the feed in this way at one side of the boiler, and behind the fire-bridge, it was thought well in these experiments to try the effect of injecting the feed directly upon the furnace crowns immediately over the fire, in order to render the experiment as trying and severe as possible. With this view, therefore, alternative dispersion pipes were arranged so as to run for a length of 3 feet 9 inches along the centre of the furnace crown and in front of the fire-bridge. The underside of each of these pipes was perforated with 32 holes set in a row. The precise arrangement of these dispersion pipes and the way in which the jets played on the furnace crowns will be seen on reference to Plate V. The pipes were varied in different experiments, and it may be of convenience, in referring to them subsequently, to call the straight one running along the side of the boiler and discharging *behind the fire-bridge*, the "*ordinary*" dispersion pipe, and the one running along the centre line of the furnace crown and discharging *directly upon it in front of the fire-bridge*, the "*experimental*" dispersion pipe. As there were two feed valves, the water could be showered either upon the left-hand furnace or the right-hand furnace as desired, or upon both at the same time.

Two glass water gauges fixed to the sides of the shell at the front end, one on the right-hand side and the other on the left. These gauges were fixed at different levels, the bottom of the right-hand glass being 2 inches below the level of the furnace crowns, and the top of the left-hand glass 2 inches above. Each glass was 18 inches long, so that the right-hand glass would give a range of 16 inches above the level of the furnace crowns, and the left-hand glass of 16 inches below it, and thus to within 2 inches of the level of the fire bars.

One brass blow-out tap, $2\frac{1}{2}$ inches in diameter, of compound gland construction.

One 7-inch dial pressure gauge, by Schaeffer and Budenberg, ranging to 150 lb., and fitted with a tell-tale finger, fixed to the front end of the boiler.

Two safety-valves; one of external pendulous dead weight construction, 3 inches in diameter; the other of the ordinary box lever type, 4 inches in diameter.

The furnace mouthpieces, as well as the fire-doors, were light, so that in the event of a collapse, and their being shot forward, they might be less destructive, and therefore the cast-iron mouthpieces and doors with which the boiler was originally equipped were exchanged for others of wrought-iron.

There were two dampers, one to each side flue.

Added to the above, there were special fittings for the conduct of the experiments.

There were three gauge rods attached to the crown of each furnace tube and carried up through the shell, passing through stuffing boxes secured thereto. The first of these was situated about 4 feet from the front end, the second 6 feet 9 inches, and the third 12 feet. These gauge rods were of iron, $\frac{3}{4}$ inch diameter, and turned up true. They were tapped into the furnace crowns and further secured with internal and external nuts. The object of these gauge rods was to show the vertical movements of the furnace tubes.

Also there were two test taps fixed to the front end plate of the boiler for ascertaining the temperature of the water at different levels, as hereinafter explained.

The general arrangements of the boiler and its connections will be better understood by a reference to Plates I., II., and III.

CHIMNEY.—The chimney to which the boiler was connected, and which had no other flue running into it, was about 72 feet high above the ground level, while the thoroughfare at the top measured 3 feet 9 inches square, giving an area of 14 square feet. The main flue between the boiler and the chimney measured 4 feet in height by 2 feet in width, the crown being semicircular, thus giving an area of 7·57 square feet. It will be seen that the size of the chimney and flue was ample for this boiler.

A glass U-shaped tube was connected to the chimney about 4 feet 6 inches above the ground level, so that the intensity of the draught could be measured in inches of water.

PROTECTIVE MEASURES : BARRICADES.—Although the yard in which the experiments were made was of good size, yet there were public thoroughfares within reach around it, and therefore it was necessary to take every precaution to prevent any mischief ensuing to persons outside the works in the event of a collapse, while it was also desirable to protect the observers so that they might conduct their operations in a place of safety, as far as that was possible. With this view the following arrangements were made :—

Firstly, a stout barricade was fixed about 12 feet in front of the boiler. The barricade measured 12 feet in width by 7 feet in height. It was faced with 3-inch deals framed to a couple of vertical posts and backed with earthwork.

Secondly, as the rush of steam and water sometimes takes a backward direction when a collapse occurs, it was thought desirable to guard against an eruption from the back of the boiler as well as from the front. With this view the top of the brickwork at the back was covered with a sheeting of 3-inch deals and then loaded with pig-iron. Added to this, a timber barricade was erected immediately behind the boiler setting, consisting of two vertical posts and a sheeting of 3-inch deals, the whole being banked up with earthwork.

Thirdly, for the protection of the observers, a wooden hut made of 3-inch deals was erected on one side of the boiler, at a distance of 33 feet, as an observatory. See Plates I., II., and III.

CONNECTIONS BETWEEN BOILER AND OBSERVATORY.—To enable the observers to operate on the boiler while under cover, the following arrangements were made:—There was fixed in the observatory a supplementary glass water gauge, as well as a supplementary dial pressure gauge, fitted with a tell-tale finger for recording the highest pressure reached. Also the feed pipes and blow-out pipes were carried through the observatory and fitted with suitable stop-valves, while cords were connected to the safety-valves. Added to this there were six graduated scales fitted with index fingers, connected by means of wire cords to the gauge rods already described as attached to the furnace crowns, so that the index fingers were in direct communication with the furnaces. By these means the observers could watch the behaviour of the furnace crowns and see how they hogged and flattened as they were heated and cooled; they could ascertain the level of the water in the boiler as well as the pressure of steam as it rose and fell, and could inject the feed or lower the water and lay bare the furnace crowns at pleasure, while, in addition, they could ease the safety-valves, blow off the steam, and reduce the pressure without leaving the observatory.

For arrangement of gauges in observatory see Plate IV.

FEED PUMP.—The water was injected by means of a feed pump having a ram 5 inches in diameter and a stroke of 12 inches, though the stroke was modified in some experiments as explained hereafter. This pump threw upwards of 5 cubic feet per minute, which is equal to the evaporation of three or four 7 feet Lancashire boilers under ordinary circumstances. It was thought well to have the pump of this capacity in order that the conditions of the experiment might be similar to those which would arise in practice, supposing one boiler in a range of three or four to become short of water and then to have the feed supply of the entire range turned into it. The pump was kept in constant work, and the delivery pipe was fitted with a relief-valve, so that when the feed-valve was closed the pump returned the water into the measuring tank. By this arrangement, directly the feed-valve was opened, the water was injected into the boiler.

MEASUREMENT OF FEED-WATER.—It was thought desirable to be able to ascertain the amount of water showered upon the furnace crowns when red-hot, and to do this a measuring tank was fixed near to the observatory. The tank, which was of cast-iron, measured 4 feet 6 inches in width, by 4 feet in breadth, and 6 feet in depth. It was supplied with water from the town's main, the supply being regulated by hand by means of a stop-valve. To measure the amount of water drawn off for charging the boiler, a glass water gauge extending from the top of the tank to the bottom was fixed to the side, and this was graduated in inches. The size of the tank was such that each inch in depth equalled $1\frac{1}{2}$ cubic feet in capacity.

OBSERVERS.—The observers engaged in the trials were Mr. Lavington E. Fletcher, Chief Engineer; Mr. George Higenbottam, Chief Engineer's Assistant; Mr. Richard Thompson, Senior Inspector; and Mr. W. H. Fowler, to whom was allotted the task of superintending the fixing of the apparatus, compiling the notes of the various observers, and assisting in preparing the report.

A programme was drawn out in preparation for each trial, and to each observer was allotted a special post, so as to prevent confusion. In taking the observations, the hour and minute at which they were taken were recorded in every case, so that they could all be reduced to one standard as regards time, and it could be seen on subsequent reference how far the various results were contemporaneous, and how far they affected one another.

Mr. John Ramsbottom, C.E., was present at one trial; Mr. Thomson, of the firm of Messrs. Crace-Calvert and Thomson, Analytical Chemists, at another; Mr. Thomas J. Richards, Engineer-Surveyor to the Board of Trade, at a third; and Mr. Charles Clayton at them all.

BEHAVIOUR OF BOILER WHEN RAISING STEAM.

As the boiler was laid down for experimental purposes, it was thought it would be well to take advantage of the opportunity to investigate other questions besides those raised with regard to the effect of turning on the feed-water when the furnace crowns were red-hot, and, therefore, a preliminary trial was made to ascertain the effect of the fire on the water with regard to its rate of heating at the surface as compared with that at the bottom, and also to ascertain the effect of the fire upon the boiler in producing movements both in the shell and furnace tubes.

For ascertaining the temperature of the water at the surface, as well as at the bottom of the boiler, two test taps were fixed to the front end-plate, one about 6 inches above the level of the furnace crowns, and the other about 3 inches above the bottom of the shell, each tap being fitted with an internal pipe extending into the boiler for a distance of about 12 feet.

For measuring the vertical movements in the shell, three wooden cross bearers were fixed a little above the crown; one at the front end, another near to the middle, and the third at the back end, the cross pieces being carried on stout uprights quite free of the brickwork setting, so as not to be affected by any movement therein. These afforded fixed datum lines from which the required measurements could be taken.

For measuring any elongation that occurred in the shell, a long wooden trammel, extending its entire length with the exception of about 3 inches at each end, was laid on the top of the brickwork setting, the pointer at one end being inserted in a small centre-punch hole, while the pointer at the other end was used as a scribe, the surface of the boiler being chalked.

In measuring the vertical movements of the furnace tubes, advantage was taken of the three gauge rods already described on page 13, which were attached to the crown of each tube and carried up through the shell, passing through stuffing boxes secured thereto.

In preparation for this preliminary experiment the boiler fires, which had been kept slowly burning for 4 days in order to dry the brickwork flues, were allowed to die out on the evening of the preceding day, and the dampers left full open all night.

At 2-20 p.m. on the day of the experiment the fires were re-lighted, the dampers being full open, and the water level 10 inches above the furnace crowns.

The draught in the chimney during this experiment was noted from time to time and found to reach $\frac{7}{16}$ inch after the fires had been burning about an hour.

The temperature of the gases at the bottom of the chimney was taken by means of one of Casartelli's pyrometers inserted through the crown of the main flue at the base of the chimney. The maximum temperature recorded during the course of the experiment was 410° F.

The temperature of the water in the boiler, both at the bottom and at the surface, was taken every few minutes, the observations of the temperature at the bottom being continued after the temperature at the surface had risen beyond 212° F. and pressure had begun to accumulate. The gradual rise of the steam pressure was also noted.

On lighting the fires at 2-20 p.m. the temperature of the water at the bottom was 78° F., and at the top, 83° F. At 3-5 p.m., 45 minutes after the fires were lighted, there was a pressure of 7 lb. of steam above the atmosphere, while the temperature of the water at the bottom had only risen to 89° F. At 3-28 p.m., 68 minutes after commencing the experiment, the steam pressure was 50 lb., while the temperature of the water at the bottom was only 103° F. In order to watch further the rate at which the temperature of the water at the bottom of the boiler rose, the fires were maintained and the steam kept up to 50 lb., the pressure at which the safety-valves commenced to blow, for about 30 minutes longer. The rise, however, took place very slowly, the last observation at 3·58 p.m.—1 hour 38 minutes after the fires were lighted, and 30 minutes after the steam had reached the blowing-off point of 50 lb.—showing a temperature of 117° F., only, although that at the top, equivalent to the pressure of steam at that time, which was 47 lb., would be 294° F., so that the difference between the temperature at the top of the water in the boiler and that at the bottom was as much as 177° F.

The following table gives a record of the observations that were taken :—

TABLE SHOWING TEMPERATURE OF WATER IN BOILER AT DIFFERENT LEVELS WHEN GETTING UP STEAM FROM COLD WATER.[1]

TIME OF OBSERVATION.	TEMPERATURE OF WATER IN BOILER.			PRESSURE IN BOILER.
	AT BOTTOM.	AT SURFACE.	DIFFERENCE.	
2·20 p.m.	78° Fahrt.	83° Fahrt.	5°	Fires lighted.
2·35 "	80° "	89° "	9°	0 lb.
2·50 "	83° "	128° "	45°	0 lb.
3·5 "	89° "	233° "	144°	7 lb.
3·20 "	97° "	267° "	170°	25 lb.
3·25 "	102° "	290° "	188°	43 lb.
3·27 "	103° "	296° "	193°	48 lb.
3·28 "	103° "	298° "	195°	50 lb.
3·30 "	104° "	298° "	194°	50 lb.
3·35 "	105° "	298° "	193°	50 lb.
3·39 "	110° "	299° "	189°	51 lb.
3·45 "	113° "	300° "	187°	52 lb.
3·58 "	117° "	294° "	177°	47 lb.

It was thought that it would be desirable to make a similar series of observations of other boilers working under the ordinary conditions of every day practice. The result of these will be found in the Appendix to this report.

---

[1] NOTE TO THE TABLE.—The temperatures in the Table above 212° were arrived at by calculation from the pressure of the steam. See Table, in D. K. Clark's Mechanical Engineers' Manual, calculated from the investigations of Regnault.

Observations of the various gauges for detecting the movement of the boiler shell and flue-tubes were taken at frequent intervals throughout the experiment and continued for about half-an-hour after the pressure of the steam had reached the blowing-off point, viz., 50 lb. These observations showed that the shell elongated $\frac{3}{4}$ inch, but that its vertical movements were slight, and certainly somewhat less than might have been expected.

The following table shows the hogging of the furnace tubes.

TABLE SHOWING HOGGING OF FURNACE TUBES WHEN GETTING UP STEAM FROM COLD WATER.

	LEFT FURNACE TUBE.				RIGHT FURNACE TUBE.		
Time of Observation.	1st Gauge, 4 ft. 6 in. from front.	2nd Gauge, 7 ft. from front.	3rd Gauge, 12 ft. from front.	Time of Observation.	1st Gauge, 4 ft. 1 in. from front.	2nd Gauge, 6 ft. 9 in. from front.	3rd Gauge, 12 ft. from front.
	Rise in 32nd of an inch.	Rise in 32nd of an inch.	Rise in 32nd of an inch.		Rise in 32nd of an inch.	Rise in 32nd of an inch.	Rise in 32nd of an inch.
2·20 p.m.	Fires lighted.	Fires lighted.	Fires lighted.	2·20 p.m.	Fires lighted.	Fires lighted.	Fires lighted.
2·26 "	2	3	3	2·27 "	2	2	2
2·31 "	4	3	4	2·33 "	3	2	3
2·37 "	6	7	8	2·38 "	4	6	5
2·42 "	9	11	12	2·43 "	9	12	13
2·46 "	10	11	14	2·47	10	14	15
2·52 "	11	13	15	2·53 "	10	14	16
3·0	11	13	16	3·1 "	11	15	18
3·5	10	12	17	3·6	11	15	19
3·10 "	10	12	17	3·11 "	10	14	18
3·15 "	9	12	17	3·16 "	10	13	18
3·22 "	8	11	17	3·23 "	10	13	16
3·27 "	6	8	12	3·29 "	7	9	12
3·33 "	4	6	10	3·35 "	6	8	11
3·38 "	4	6	9	3·40 "	6	8	10
3·45 "	4	5	8	3·46 "	6	7	9
3·50 "	4	5	8	3·51	5	6	9
3·56 "	3	4	8	3·57 "	5	6	8

It will be seen from the Table that at a distance of 12 feet from the front, or at about mid-length of the furnace tube, the maximum hogging was upwards of $\frac{1}{2}$ inch in both tubes.

This will show the importance of allowing sufficient space between the bottom of the gusset stays and the crown of the furnace tube, in Lancashire and Cornish boilers, so that the end plate at that part may be elastic, and be able, as it were, to breathe in and out as the furnace may require. Otherwise, grooving in the neighbourhood of the furnace mouth, at which a hinging action takes place, and straining generally, is likely to occur. This hogging also shows the inexpediency of tying the furnace tubes to the shell at about the middle of their length with a view to supporting them. The support is unnecessary: the tie is objectionable.

The movements of the furnaces will be more clearly understood on reference to the diagrams given on Plate VI. The left-hand portion of the diagrams, which illustrates the behaviour of the furnace crowns between the times 2-20 p.m. and 3-56 p.m., shows the hogging when steam was being got up from cold water. The right-hand portion of the diagram, which illustrates the behaviour of the furnace crowns from 4-55 p.m. to 5-28 p.m., will be referred to hereafter.

These preliminary observations regarding the behaviour of the boiler when steam was being got up having been made, the experiments for ascertaining the effect of showering cold water on to the red-hot furnace crowns were at once proceeded with.

RED-HOT FURNACE CROWN EXPERIMENTS, No. 1 AND No. 1A.

On considering the mode of conducting these experiments it was seen there was a difficulty in ascertaining the right moment to inject the feed. If the feed were injected before the furnace crowns were red-hot it would not be a full test, and, on the other hand, if the injection were deferred too long the furnace crowns might be overheated and weakened to so great an extent in the interval as to collapse from steam-pressure alone, and thus defeat the experiment.

To determine when the furnace crowns were red-hot was by no means easy. To watch them from the fire-door was impracticable under steam-pressure on account of the danger involved. It was therefore thought it would be well to make the first trial at atmospheric pressure as a guide to the best mode of conducting further experiments, while it would also help to settle the question previously raised,—whether showering the cold feed on to overheated furnace crowns would cause so sudden and violent a contraction as to rend them transversely, in the same way as the shells of boilers are sometimes rent at the bottom through the introduction of the feed at too low a level.

With this view, therefore, the following experiment was made, the feed being injected at atmospheric pressure instead of under steam pressure, as in subsequent trials.

EXPERIMENT No. 1.—At 4-26 p.m. on the same day that the preliminary observations previously recorded had been made, the blow-out tap was opened full bore, the water at the time standing at 8¼ inches above the furnace crowns, and the safety valves being propped open.

By 4-45 p.m., 19 minutes after the blow-out tap was opened, the water was brought down to the level of the furnace crowns, when the blow-out tap was shut.

The fires were then worked up into good condition, the safety-valves being kept open.

At 4-50 p.m. the blow-out tap was again opened full bore, and kept so until 5-10 p.m., when the water was brought down to 16 inches below the level of the furnace crowns and about 2 inches above the level of the firebars.

At 5-15 p.m., 25 minutes after the water had begun to leave the furnace crowns, the dead-weight safety-valve was closed, but by oversight the lever safety-valve was left open. At the same moment the feed was showered on to both furnace crowns, immediately over the fire, by means of two "*experimental*" dispersion pipes, the temperature of the feed-water being 62° F., and the rate of injection as nearly as may be 5½ cubic feet per minute.

On this being done, the pressure of steam in the boiler rose from 6 lb. to 12 lb. in 1¼ minutes. The injection of the feed was kept on continuously and in 1¾ minutes the pressure fell down to 1 lb.

EXPERIMENT No. 1A.—As the lever safety-valve had been inadvertently left open, it was decided to repeat the experiment, and the fires were therefore worked up again.

At 5-42 p.m., both safety-valves being open, the surface of the water on a level with the furnace crowns and the steam pressure 3 lb., the blow-out tap was opened full bore.

At 5-54 p.m. the blow-out tap was shut, the water having been brought down to 16 inches below the level of the furnace crowns, and about 2 inches above the level of the firebars.

At 5-56 p.m., 14 minutes after the water had begun to leave the furnace crowns, both safety-valves were closed and the feed turned on full bore, and showered on to both furnace crowns, immediately over the fire, as before, the fires being about 7 inches thick, clear and bright, and the dampers full open.

As soon as the feed was turned on the pressure in the boiler began to rise. In $\frac{3}{4}$ of a minute it rose from 6 lb. to 27 lb., after which it gradually fell.

The injection of the feed was kept on continuously. In 18½ minutes the pressure was again reduced to 6 lb., and in 20 minutes the water was brought up again to the level of the furnace crowns, while the pressure of steam was 4 lb.

The boiler was so thoroughly heated at this test that two blisters, one measuring about 20 inches by 9 inches, and the other 10 inches by 6 inches, were developed on the crown of the shell over the left-hand furnace.

Diagrams showing the movements of the furnaces when they were laid bare, gradually overheated, and then subjected to a shower of cold water, will be found on Plate VI. The right-hand portion, illustrating the behaviour of the furnace crowns from 4-55 p.m. to 5-28 p.m., refers to the movements in question.

On examining the furnaces after the test, the plates were seen to be severely sprung at each of the ring seams of rivets over the fire, and on gauging the tubes it was found that the greatest distortion had occurred at the third ring seam of rivets in the right-hand furnace tube situated at a distance of about 7 feet 6 inches from the front end. The furnace tube at this point measured 3 feet 1¼ inches horizontally by 2 feet 9¾ inches vertically, showing that the tube was as much as 3½ inches oval.

The furnace, however, was not rent by sudden contraction on the injection of the feed, as it had been suggested it might be, nor was an ungovernable amount of pressure suddenly generated. The shell was not rent or injured, nor was the pressure of steam sufficient even to make the safety-valves blow. They were loaded to 50 lb., and the pressure only reached 27 lb. With the exception of the flattening of the furnace crowns and straining of the seams of rivets, there was no injury to the boiler, nor was the setting disturbed in any way.

RED-HOT FURNACE CROWN EXPERIMENT No. 2.

In preparation for this experiment, the first four crown plates in each furnace, which had been injured in Trial No. 1, were taken out and re-rolled, so as to restore them to their circular shape, after which they were put in their place and riveted up afresh. This being done, the boiler was tested by hydraulic pressure up to 100 lb. on the inch, when the furnace tubes proved tight, and on being gauged showed no movement.

The difficulty of ascertaining the right moment at which to inject the feed upon the furnace crowns has already been mentioned, and it was attempted to meet this in the following way.

The opinion was entertained that at the commencement of the collapse of a furnace tube the movement was gradual, so that warning would be given. Such was the case in an explosion which occurred at Salford on the 18th of August, 1884, when the engineman's attention was called to the furnace by a hissing noise, and, on looking in, he saw that the crown was gradually coming down, whereon he commenced to draw the fire, but had scarcely finished when the rupture occurred. Particulars will be found in the Report on Preliminary Inquiry No. 89 under the Boiler Explosions Act. Relying on warning being given, it was thought that by carefully watching the three index fingers in the observatory connected to the furnaces the impending collapse could be sufficiently anticipated to allow time to turn on the feed. With this view an observer was stationed to watch the index fingers continuously, and to give notice of the first indication of approaching collapse. Added to this, at the suggestion of Mr. John Ramsbottom, C.E., a fusible disc was bolted to each furnace crown and one of the gauge rods screwed into it, so that when the furnace crown became overheated the disc would be melted and the gauge rod liberated, thereby giving warning in the observatory, by the movement of the index fingers and the sudden falling of the counter-balance weight attached thereto, that the time had come, or, at all events, was approaching, for turning on the feed.

Also two strips of sheet lead about $1\frac{1}{2}$ inches wide and $\frac{1}{16}$ inch thick were laid upon each furnace crown, one about 4 feet and the other 6 feet from the front end of the boiler. The object of these lead strips was to afford additional evidence of the overheating of the furnace crowns.

At 12·0 noon the fires were lighted, the boiler being filled with water at a temperature of 62° F. up to 8 inches above the level of the furnace crowns, and by 1-19 p.m. the steam was raised to a pressure of 50 lb.

During the time steam was being raised, observations of the temperature of the water at the top and at the bottom, as well as of the movements in the shell and furnace tubes, were recorded as in the prior experiments. These results were found to corroborate very closely those already reported, and it is therefore not necessary to repeat them here.

These observations having been made, the steam in the boiler was allowed to escape till the pressure fell to 10 lb., at which point the safety-valves were then adjusted to blow-off.

At 1-49 p.m., when the water was 6 inches above the level of the furnace crowns with brisk fires burning and the dampers wide open, the blow-out tap was opened full bore.

By 1-53 p.m. the water was brought down to the level of the furnace crowns.

By 1-57 it was brought down to 15 inches below the level of the furnace crowns, and about 3 inches above the level of the fire-bars. At this point the blow-out tap was shut. The fires were allowed to go on burning with the furnace crowns bare, and the observers watched the index fingers of the gauge rods in the observatory in order to note the behaviour of the furnace crowns.

The observers relied upon the fusible discs to give warning as soon as the furnaces were thoroughly overheated, but in this they were disappointed. The index fingers attached thereto continued to show a progressive hogging, till at 2-3 p.m., *i.e.*, 10 minutes after the water had been brought down to the level of the furnace crowns, and 6 minutes after it had been brought down to within 3 inches of the level of the fire-bars, the index fingers of the gauges, which were not fitted with fusible discs but attached directly to the furnace crown, indicated a retrograde movement on the part of the right-hand furnace, showing that it was beginning to come down. The instant this was detected the order was given to turn on the feed, but the valve was scarcely opened before the right-hand furnace tube collapsed and rent.

It would seem that the collapse had already begun before the valve was opened, and that the feed was not introduced soon enough. This was the view taken of it at the time, and it is thought that subsequent experiments corroborated it.

The furnace rent at the first ring seam immediately over the fire, forming an opening measuring about 3 feet circumferentially by 12 inches wide at the middle. Through this opening the steam and water rushed out in a torrent of great violence, dashing against the barricade in front of the boiler, scattering the coal lying there, and shooting portions of it against the feed tank with considerable force, though this was directly at right angles to the line of fire and at a distance of 35 feet. Some of the coal was showered into the tank and caused inconvenience at a subsequent experiment by choking the pump. The upper portion of the firebridge was shot backwards and swept along the external flue beneath the boiler until it reached the cross wall at the front. But neither the furnace mouthpiece nor fire-door were blown out of place, nor was the boiler stirred from its seat or otherwise damaged. The left-hand furnace tube was not visibly distorted, but, on gauging it subsequently, the second and third belts of plating were found to be bulged down about 1 inch at the crown.

For sketch of the collapsed flue-tube see Plate VII.

It was a matter of surprise to the observers that the index fingers attached to the fusible discs had given no warning of the overheating of the furnace crowns, but on entering the boiler after the experiment the reason for this was apparent. The fusible disc on each furnace crown had melted, and had fallen to the bottom of the boiler in the form of shot. The lead strips also had melted and severed at the centre, and they also had fallen to the bottom of the boiler. The reason that no indication was given of the melting of the fusible discs was found to be that the gauge rods attached to them had hung in the stuffing boxes, the counter-weight in the observatory not having been heavy enough to overcome the friction.

It will be seen from this experiment that in some cases at all events, a furnace crown when overheated may collapse with very little or no prior warning, and that when the whole of the upper half of the furnace tube is overheated, as in this case, the collapse when once it begins is but the work of an instant, so that to stand before a furnace in order to draw the fires when shortness of water has occurred, relying on the gradual movement of the crown to give timely warning, is a very hazardous undertaking.

RED-HOT FURNACE CROWN EXPERIMENTS, No. 3 AND No. 3A.

In preparation for a further experiment, the first thing to be done was to correct the gauges attached to the discs, so as to prevent their sticking in future. With this purpose the rods $\frac{3}{4}$ inch diameter were removed, and wires $\frac{1}{8}$ inch diameter substituted for them. Added to this, the connection inside the boiler to the disc was made by means of a chain, so as to be flexible, while a counterbalance weight was fixed to the top of the chain, by which means the wire could be worked up and down at any time through the stuffing box by hand, to see that it was free and in working order.

Further, it was thought it would be well to vary the mode of laying bare the furnace crowns, and to do this by gradual evaporation rather than by drawing off the water at the blow-out tap. It is by evaporation that furnace crowns are generally laid bare in actual work. The attendant mis-reads his glass water gauge and omits to feed his boiler, in consequence of which the water level is gradually lowered and the furnace crowns laid bare.

It is true that sometimes a blow-out tap is opened full bore and found to stick fast, so that it cannot be shut, and sometimes it is left open by oversight, but in the majority of cases the furnace crowns are laid bare by gradual evaporation. It was determined, therefore, to lay bare the furnace crowns by evaporation instead of by drawing the water off at the blow-out tap, as in Experiment No. 2.

Further, this mode of operation afforded an opportunity of feeling the way step by step to the right moment for turning on the feed, in the following manner:—The water could be brought down to the level of the furnace crowns, and the fires kept burning briskly for 5 minutes, and then the feed could be turned on. If no injury resulted either to furnace crowns or boiler from this treatment, the experiment could be repeated with an interval of 10 minutes between bringing the water down to the level of the furnace crowns and turning on the feed; and if no injury then resulted, the experiment could be repeated with a still longer interval, say of 15 minutes, and so on.

EXPERIMENT No. 3.—In preparation for this experiment the fires were kept burning all the previous day. At the commencement steam was raised to 30 lb., at which pressure the safety-valves were adjusted to blow-off.

At 1-28 p.m. the blow-out tap was opened full bore, the water being 3 inches above the level of the furnace crowns, the pressure of steam 35 lb. on the inch, and the safety-valves blowing hard.

By 1-31½ p.m. the water was brought down to the level of the furnace crowns, and the blow-out tap was shut. The fires were burning briskly, 7 inches thick, the dampers full open, and the pressure of steam 36 lb.

At 1-36½ p.m., 5 minutes after the water was brought down to the level of the furnace crowns, the feed was turned on through the left-hand feed valve, fitted with an "*ordinary*" dispersion pipe *(see Plate V.)*, the right-hand valve being shut. The temperature of the feed was 61° F., and the rate of injection 5 cubic feet per minute. There was however no increase of pressure.

On examining the furnace tubes from the fire door after the experiment, they did not appear to be bulged or otherwise injured.

EXPERIMENT No. 3A.—As no injury resulted either to furnace crowns or boiler in the last experiment, it was proposed to repeat it, and this was done the same day, with this modification, that the interval between bringing the water down to the level of the furnace crowns and turning on the feed, was extended from 5 minutes to 10 minutes.

At 1-53 p.m. the blow-out tap was opened full bore, the water being 1½ inches above the furnace crowns, and the pressure of steam 34 lb.

By 1-54½ p.m. the water was brought down to the level of the furnace crowns, and the blow-out tap was shut, the fires being 6 inches thick, burning briskly, with dampers full open, and steam at a pressure of 36 lb.

At 2-2 p.m., $7\frac{1}{2}$ minutes after the water was brought down to the level of the furnace crowns, the pump was suddenly brought to a standstill in consequence of the derangement of one of the wheels on the driving shaft. This put the observers somewhat in a dilemma. The furnace crowns were bare, the fires were burning briskly, and the feed could not be injected, while as $7\frac{1}{2}$ minutes had elapsed since the water had been brought down to the level of the furnace crowns, it was thought it would be dangerous to stand in front of the boiler to draw the fires. Under these circumstances it was thought the most prudent course would be to shut down the dampers and lift the safety-valves, so as to blow off the steam. This was therefore done, and in 8 minutes the pressure was reduced from 36 lb. to 12 lb.

At 2-10 p.m. it was found possible to start the pump again, and the feed was turned on, the water in the boiler being 3 inches below the level of the furnace crowns, when the pressure of steam began at once to fall, and in the course of 13 minutes was reduced to Zero.

Shortly after this the pump failed again, and on examination it was found that several pieces of coal, which had been shot into the tank by the torrent of water that ensued on the collapse which occurred in Experiment No. 2, had choked the suction valve. This brought the experiment to an end.

RED-HOT FURNACE CROWN EXPERIMENTS No. 4 AND No. 4A.

EXPERIMENT No. 4.—In conducting this experiment it was proposed to take up the thread at the point at which it had been broken off during the progress of experiment No. 3A by the breakdown of the feed pump.

At 1-45 p.m. the blow-out tap was opened, the water in the boiler standing 5 inches above the level of the furnace crowns.

By 1-52 p.m. the water was brought down to the level of the furnace crowns, and the blow-out tap was shut, the fires being 7 inches thick, the dampers full open, and the draught gauge shewing a pull in the chimney equal to a column of water of $\frac{3}{4}$ inch, while the steam pressure was 25 lb. on the inch with the safety valves blowing.

At 2-2 p.m., 10 minutes after the water was brought down to the level of the furnace crowns, the feed was turned on full bore through the left-hand feed valve, fitted with an "*ordinary*" dispersion pipe *(see Plate V.)*, the right-hand valve being shut. The temperature of the feed was 44° F., and the rate of injection $2\frac{1}{2}$ cubic feet per minute. There was, however, no sudden rise in pressure. On the contrary it at once began to fall, and by 2-5 p.m., 3 minutes after the feed was turned on, the pressure was only 19 lb.

As neither the furnace crowns nor the boiler were injured, the water was pumped up to about 3 inches above the level of the furnace crowns, and the fires again got under way for the next experiment.

It will be observed that the rate of injection was less than on prior occasions. This arose from the stroke of the pump having been reduced, as some fears were entertained with regard to the strength of the shafting.

EXPERIMENT No. 4A.—This experiment was made on the same day and under the same conditions as No. 4, excepting that the interval between bringing the water down to the level of the furnace crowns and turning on the feed was extended from 10 minutes to 15 minutes.

At 2-30 p.m. the blow-out tap was opened, the water standing at $1\frac{3}{4}$ inches above the level of the furnace crowns.

By 2-33 p.m. the water was brought down to the level of the furnace crowns, and the blow-out tap was shut, the fires being from 7 to 8 inches thick, the dampers full open, the draught gauge indicating $\frac{7}{16}$ inch of water, and the steam pressure being 25 lb. with the safety valves blowing.

At 2-48 p.m., 15 minutes after the water had been brought down to the level of the furnace crowns, the feed was turned on full bore through the left-hand feed valve, fitted with an "*ordinary*" dispersion pipe *(see Plate V.)*, the right-hand valve being shut. The temperature of the water was 44° F., and the rate of injection 2 cubic feet per minute. There was, however, no sudden increase of pressure on injecting the feed. On the contrary it began to fall, and in 7 minutes afterwards the pressure was only 20 lb.

RED-HOT FURNACE CROWN EXPERIMENTS Nos. 5, 5A, 5B, AND 5C.

EXPERIMENT No. 5.—In experiments No. 4 and No. 4A the rate of injection of the feed, as then explained, was only half what it had been on prior occasions, the stroke of the pump having been reduced on account of some fears that were entertained with regard to the safety of the shafting which drove it.

In order to meet this, an additional bearing was fixed close to the pump crank, so as to reduce the overhang. This enabled the original stroke of 12 inches to be resorted to again, and brought the rate of discharge up to about 5 cubic feet per minute, as before, which is nearly equal to the evaporation of four Lancashire boilers 7 feet in diameter. In other respects Experiment No. 5 was made under the same conditions as No. 4 and No. 4A.

The pressure at which the safety-valves began to blow was 25 lb. per square inch.

At 12-8 p.m. the blow-out tap was opened full bore, the water standing 6 inches above the level of the furnace crowns.

By 12-12 p.m. the water was brought down to the level of the furnace crowns, and the blow-out tap was shut, the fires being 8 inches thick, the dampers full open, the draught gauge at the base of the chimney indicating $\frac{7}{16}$ inch of water, the steam pressure being 27 lb. on the inch, and both safety-valves blowing hard.

In prior experiments it had been thought desirable to retire from the front of the boiler as soon as the water was brought down to the level of the furnace crowns; but, having gained increased confidence in the conduct of the experiments, the observers ventured to stand before the boiler and give the fires another charge, although the furnace crowns were beginning to be laid bare. By this means the intensity of the fires was the better maintained to the end of the experiment.

By 12-22 p.m., or 10 minutes after the water had been brought down to the level of the furnace crowns, it was lowered 2 inches, thus laying the furnace crowns bare for a width of 16 inches. At this point the feed was turned on full bore through the left-hand feed-valve, fitted with an "*ordinary*" dispersion pipe *(see Plate V.)*, the right-hand valve being shut. The temperature of the feed was 47° F., the rate of injection 5 cubic feet per minute, and the pressure of steam 26½ lb., the safety-valves blowing hard. There was, however, no rise of pressure; on the contrary, it began to fall, and by 12-23 p.m., one minute afterwards, it was reduced to 25½ lb.

On looking into the furnaces at the close of the experiment, no signs of leakage or straining could be seen.

EXPERIMENT No. 5A.—This experiment was made on the same day and under the same conditions as No. 5, excepting that the interval between bringing the water down to the level of the furnace crowns and turning on the feed was extended from 10 minutes to 15 minutes.

At 12-45 p.m. the blow-out tap was opened full bore, the water standing at 3 inches above the level of the furnace crowns.

By 12-47½ p.m. the water was brought down to the level of the furnace crowns, when the blow-out tap was shut, the fires being 9 inches thick, the dampers full open, the draught gauge at the base of the chimney indicating nearly ½ inch of water, the steam pressure being 28 lb., and both safety valves blowing hard. After the blow-out tap was shut, the fires were charged the last thing before retiring from the front of the boiler.

By 1-2½ p.m., or 15 minutes after the water had been brought down to the level of the furnace crowns, it was lowered 2¾ inches, thus laying the furnace crowns bare for a width of 19 inches. At this point the feed was turned on full bore through the left-hand feed-valve, fitted with an "*ordinary*" dispersion pipe *(see Plate V.)*, the right-hand valve being shut. The temperature of the feed was 47° F., the rate of injection 5⅓ cubic feet per minute, the pressure of steam 28½ lb., and the safety-valves blowing hard. There was, however, no rise of pressure. On the contrary, it at once began to fall, and by 1-4 p.m. was reduced to 27 lb.

The maximum steam pressure during this trial was 30 lb., at which point it remained from 12-56 p.m. to 12-58 p.m.

On looking into the furnaces after the experiment, no signs of straining or distortion were visible.

EXPERIMENT No. 5B.—This experiment was made on the same day as No. 5 and No. 5A. The feed, however, instead of being injected through an "*ordinary*" dispersion pipe on the left-hand side of the boiler, and on one side of the furnaces, was injected through an "*experimental*" dispersion pipe *(see Plate V.)*, which showered the water directly on to the right-hand furnace crown immediately over the fire.

At 1-51 p.m. the blow-out tap was opened full bore, the water in the boiler standing 6½ inches above the level of the furnace crown.

By 1-56½ p.m. the water was brought down to the level of the furnace crowns, when the blow-out tap was shut, the fires being 9 inches thick, the dampers full open, the draught gauge in the chimney indicating nearly ½ inch of water, the steam pressure being 28 lb., and both safety-valves blowing hard. After the blow-out tap was shut, the fires were charged the last thing before retiring from the front of the boiler.

At 2-6½ p.m., or 10 minutes after the water had been brought down to the level of the furnace crowns, it was lowered 1½ inches, thus laying the furnace crowns bare for a width of 14 inches. At this point the feed was turned on full bore through the "*experimental*" dispersion pipe mentioned above, the temperature of the feed being 47° F., the rate of injection 5⅞ cubic feet per minute, the pressure of steam 31 lb., and the safety-valves blowing hard. There was, however, no rise of pressure. On the contrary, it at once began to fall, and by 2-7½ p.m. was reduced to 30 lb.

The maximum pressure during the trial was 31 lb. at 2-6½ p.m.

On looking into the furnaces after the experiment a slight leakage was detected at the crown of the second and third seams in the right-hand furnace, but there was no appearance of distortion.

EXPERIMENT No. 5c.—This experiment was made on the same day and under the same conditions as No. 5B, excepting that it was proposed to extend the interval between laying bare the furnace crowns and turning on the feed, from 10 minutes to 15 minutes.

At 2-25 p.m. the blow-out tap was opened full bore, the water standing 2½ inches above the level of the furnace crowns.

By 2-28 p.m. the water was brought down to the level of the furnace crowns, when the blow-out tap was shut, the fires being 9 inches thick, the dampers full open, the draught gauge in the chimney indicating nearly ½ inch of water, the steam pressure being 29½ lb., and the safety-valves blowing hard. After the blow-out tap was shut, the fires were charged the last thing before retiring from the front of the boiler.

At 2-42 p.m., or 14 minutes after the water had been brought down to the level of the furnace crowns, the movement of the index finger in the observatory indicated that the tin disc on the left furnace crown had melted. On this the feed was at once turned on through the "experimental" dispersion pipe (see Plate V.), which showered the water directly on to the right-hand furnace crown, the left-hand valve being shut. The temperature of the feed was 47° F., the rate of injection 5½ cubic feet per minute, the steam pressure 28 lb. on the inch, and the safety-valves were blowing hard. At the moment that the feed was injected the water in the boiler had been brought down 2¾ inches below the level of the furnace crowns, thus laying them bare for a width of 19 inches. There was, however, no rise of pressure on the injection of the feed. On the contrary, it at once began to fall, and by 2-43½ p.m. was reduced to 27 lb.

The maximum pressure during the experiment was 31 lb. At this point it remained stationary from 2-32 p.m. to 2-37 p.m.

On looking into the furnaces after the experiment a slight leakage was observed at the ring seams in each furnace.

On making a more detailed examination of the boiler after it had been emptied and laid off, the following observations were made.

In the left-hand furnace there were distinct signs of overheating on the fire side at the crown of the first, second, third, and fourth belts of plating for a width of 18 to 20 inches circumferentially. The plates were of a rusty colour and quite free from soot. The discolouration commenced at about midway in the first plate and died out at about midway on the fourth plate, just over the fire-bridge.

In the right-hand furnace tube there were also signs of overheating on the fire side at the crown of the second, third, and fourth belts of plating, but the discolouration was not so clear and distinct as in the left furnace tube, excepting on the fourth belt of plating immediately over the fire-bridge, which was distinctly discoloured for a width of about 6 inches.

On examining the boiler internally it was found that both of the lead strips which were laid across the second and third belts of plating in the left-hand furnace had melted through at the middle, and fallen to the bottom of the boiler. The tin disc attached to this furnace tube was also partly fused, sufficiently so to allow it to be drawn over the heads of the three brass set screws by which it was secured to the furnace crown. The lead strip on the right-hand furnace tube on the second belt of plating had also melted through at the middle, separated, and fallen to the bottom of the boiler. But the lead strip on the third belt of plating, which was immediately under the dispersion pipe, was only partially fused through, and not separated. The lead disc on the right-hand furnace tube, which was also immediately under the dispersion pipe, was partially fused. A considerable quantity of granulated lead and tin was found lying at the bottom of the boiler, along with the fragments of the lead strips.

Drawings showing the extent to which the fusible discs were melted will be found on Plate IX.

Red-Hot Furnace Crown Experiment No. 6.

The previous experiment was the first occasion on which the fusible disc had given warning of the overheating of the furnace crown. It was thought highly probable, as there was an interval of only 14 minutes between lowering the water to the level of the furnace crowns and the warning given by the index finger in the observatory, whereas the fires had previously run for 15 minutes after the water was brought down to that level, that the fusible discs had been partially melted during experiments Nos. 5, 5A, and 5B, and therefore that it would be well to repeat experiment No. 5c with new fusible discs.

As the last experiment had shown that the disc could be trusted to give warning of the overheating of the furnace crowns, it was thought it would be well to carry on the next experiment till the disc melted and gave warning by the falling of the counterbalance weight, instead of limiting it to a given number of minutes. With this view experiment No. 6 was instituted, the lead and tin discs being reinstated as before, and also two lead strips laid across each furnace crown.

The pressure at which the safety valves began to blow was 25 lb. per square inch.

At 1·20 p.m. the blow-out tap was opened full bore, the water standing at 6¼ inches above the level of the furnace crowns.

By 1·25¼ p.m. the water was brought down to the level of the furnace crowns, when the blow-out tap was shut, the fires being 9 inches thick, the dampers full open, the draught gauge in the chimney indicating nearly ½ inch of water, the steam pressure being 28 lb., and both safety-valves blowing hard. After the blow-out tap was shut the fires were charged the last thing before retiring from the front of the boiler.

At 1-43 p.m., 17½ minutes from the time the water was level with the furnace crowns, the counterbalance weight in the observatory connected to the tin disc attached to the left hand furnace crown suddenly fell, showing that the disc had melted and become disengaged from the furnace crown. On this signal the feed was at once turned on through the right-hand feed valve, fitted with an " *experimental* " dispersion pipe *(see Plate V.)* which showered the water directly upon the right-hand furnace crown, the left-hand valve being shut. By this time the water in the boiler had fallen 3 inches, thus laying the furnace crowns bare for a width of 20 inches. The temperature of the feed was 50° F., the rate of injection 5·2 cubic feet per minute, the pressure of steam 31 lb., and the safety-valves were blowing hard. There was however no rise of pressure. On the contrary, it at once began to fall, and by 1-44 p.m. it was reduced to 28 lb.

The maximum pressure during the experiment was 31 lb. from 1-37 p.m. to 1-43 p.m.

On examining the boiler after it had been emptied, it was found that both the lead and tin discs were partially fused, while each of the four lead strips laid across the furnace crowns was completely melted away at the middle for 8 or 9 inches. There were, however, no very definite signs that the plates of the furnace crowns had been red-hot. They were not discoloured, but all along the crowns of both furnaces on the fire side the hard soot was burnt off in places.

Drawings showing the extent to which the fusible discs were melted will be found on Plate IX.

Red-hot Furnace Crown Experiment No. 7.

As the temperature at which tin or lead, of which the fusible discs were made, will melt is very much below a red heat, the question will arise, how far did they give an indication that the furnace crowns had actually been red-hot.

When lead is placed in a ladle over a fire, its own weight keeps it in contact with the bottom of the ladle. The lead discs, however, in the experimental boiler were suspended by a wire cord, as shown in Plate IX., which tended to draw them away from the furnace crown.

As soon, therefore, as the disc began to fuse, the melted portion ran away, and contact between the disc and the furnace crown ceased. The remainder of the melting had to be done mainly by radiation, the disc had, as it were, to be toasted away, and that had to go on until the disc was sufficiently wasted round the three bolts by which it was secured to the furnace crown to allow it to pass over the bolt heads and escape. A reference to Plate IX. will give a better idea of the extent to which they were wasted than a mere description, and when all the circumstances of the case are considered, it is thought that the condition of the fusible discs warrants the conclusion that the furnace crowns had been heated very much above the melting point of lead; in fact that they had been red-hot. Still, however, positive proof was lacking, and this was unsatisfactory. Messrs. Crace-Calvert and Thomson, of Manchester, the well-known analytical chemists, were therefore requested to furnish if possible an alloy that would not melt at a lower temperature than a red heat. To meet this Messrs. Crace-Calvert and Thomson instituted a series of experiments and furnished several alloy plugs.

On the receipt of these plugs, after they had been turned and chased, it was thought well to test them experimentally, along with discs of tin, lead, and zinc, before adopting them in the boiler; subjecting them as nearly as may be to the same conditions as they would be subjected to in the boiler itself.

For this purpose the following apparatus was arranged:—The fusible discs or alloy plugs to be experimented on were attached to a wrought-iron plate, just as they would be to the furnace crowns of the boiler. The plate was laid over a small coke fire, 18 inches in diameter, used as a brass furnace, a cord being attached to the fusible discs and alloy plugs, and carried over pulleys to a counterbalance weight, so as to draw them away from the plate. This was just a counterpart arrangement to that adopted in the boiler. See Plate VIII.

The result was that the tin disc was liberated in 3 minutes, though the wrought-iron plate was not visibly heated. The lead disc was liberated in $4\frac{1}{2}$ minutes, and the wrought-iron plate heated to a dull red. The zinc disc was liberated in 10 minutes, and the wrought-iron plate heated to a cherry red. Also two alloy plugs, both of the same composition, were tried. One of them was severed in $5\frac{1}{4}$ minutes and the other in $6\frac{1}{4}$ minutes, the wrought-iron plate being heated to a dull red in the first case, and a blood-red in the second.

It will be observed that although the melting point of zinc is between 700° and 800° F., yet the discs, when attached to the plate in the way described, were not liberated till the plate was heated to a cherry red. There could, therefore, be little doubt that the furnace crowns in the boiler would have to be red-hot before the zinc discs would be liberated. Under these circumstances, and further, as there appeared more or less uncertainty about the behaviour of the alloy plugs, it was thought better to adopt zinc discs in the next experiment, and this was, therefore, done.

Drawings showing the extent to which the fusible discs were melted in the experiments just referred to will be found on Plate VIII.

Added to the zinc discs, two plugs were screwed into each furnace crown, one of lead, the other of tin, so that warning might be given of the gradual overheating of the plates. These plugs were connected by means of wire cords to index fingers traversing graduated scales in the observatory, and kept taut by a counterbalance weight just as in the case of the fusible discs already described. In addition to the fusible discs and plugs, a strip of lead, 4 feet in length by $1\frac{1}{2}$ inch in width and $\frac{1}{16}$ inch in thickness, was laid across the middle of each of the first 8 belts of plating, to serve as an index, after the experiment, of the extent to which the plates had been heated.

The precise position of the fusible discs and plugs, as well as the method of attachment, will be seen on reference to Plates IX. and X.

With these preliminary explanations, a description of experiment No. 7 may now be given.

In preparation for this experiment the fires in the boiler had been kept burning for about two days, so that the flues might be warm and the draught good.

The experiment was commenced at 6-0 p.m. when the fires were roused, the steam pressure gauge standing at zero, and the water being $9\frac{1}{2}$ inches above the level of the furnace crowns.

At 6-23 p.m. both safety-valves, which were loaded to 25 lb. on the inch, began to blow.

At 6-30 p.m. the blow-out tap was opened full bore, the water in the boiler standing $9\frac{1}{2}$ inches above the level of the furnace crowns.

By 6-38 p.m. the water was brought down to the level of the furnace crowns, when the blow-out tap was shut. To secure the intensity of the fires being preserved as long as possible, they were re-charged after this, though the water was beginning to leave the furnace crowns. This being done, the observers withdrew from the front of the boiler, leaving the fires 9 inches thick and burning briskly, with the dampers full open and the draught gauge showing a pull in the chimney equal to a column of water of nearly $\frac{1}{2}$ inch. The pressure of steam by this time had risen to $29\frac{1}{2}$ lb., and both safety-valves were blowing-off fiercely.

At 6-56 p.m., 18 minutes after the water was brought down to the level of the furnace crowns, the falling of one of the counterbalance weights, and the movement of the index finger in the observatory, indicated that the lead plug on the left-hand furnace had melted.

At 6-59 p.m., 21 minutes after the water was brought down to the level of the furnace crowns, the falling of another counterbalance weight indicated that the tin plug on the left furnace had melted.

At 7-1½ p.m., 23½ minutes after the water was brought down to the level of the furnace crowns, the falling of another counterbalance weight indicated that the zinc disc on the right-hand furnace had melted. On this being observed, the feed was at once turned on through the right-hand feed-valve fitted with an "*experimental*" dispersion pipe *(see Plate V.)*, which showered the water directly upon the right-hand furnace crown, the left-hand valve being shut. The water level at the time was 3⅝ inches below the crown, thus laying bare a strip of plating about 21 inches wide, while the temperature of the feed was 60° F., the rate of injection a little more than 4½ cubic feet per minute, the pressure of steam 28½ lb., and the safety-valves blowing freely.

Showering the feed-water at a temperature of 60° F. on to the red-hot furnace crown was not attended with any sudden increase of pressure. On the contrary, the pressure at once began to fall and in 2½ minutes it had fallen from 28½ lb. to 26 lb., when the safety-valves were opened and the pressure further relieved.

At 7-3½ p.m., 2 minutes after the water had been showered on to the right-hand furnace, the falling of another counterbalance weight indicated that the zinc disc on the left-hand furnace had melted.

The rate at which the pressure rose and fell during the experiment will be best seen by a reference to the diagram on Plate XI.

On looking into the furnaces the ring seams over the fire were seen to be leaking freely. The crown of both furnace tubes was discoloured on the fire side, the discolouration extending for a width of about 12 inches, and a length of 8 feet in the left furnace, and 9 feet in the right furnace. The line of demarcation between the portion of the tube which had been overheated, and that which had not, was quite distinct, the sides and haunches of the tube being coated with soot, while the crown was quite bare and of a brick-red colour.

On making an examination the following morning, it was found that the overlaps of the first seven ring seams in each furnace were sprung at the crown; but the shape of the furnace tubes was practically unaltered, though the right-hand tube was slightly bulged in three places. Two of these bulges were situated at the crown of the second belt of plating, one measuring 12 inches by 7 inches by $\frac{1}{4}$ inch deep at the middle, and the other 12 inches by 9 inches by $\frac{3}{16}$ inch deep at the middle. The third bulge was situated just at the crown of the third ring seam, and measured 11 inches by 10 inches by $\frac{1}{32}$ inch deep at the middle. It was also seen that all the fusible discs and plugs on both furnace crowns had melted. But the gauge wires attached to the tin and lead plugs on the right-hand furnace had hung in the stuffing boxes, which accounted for no warning being received in the observatory of the melting of these plugs during the test, though warning was received of the melting of the others. It was also seen that the first five lead strips laid across the crown of the left-hand furnace tube, as well as the first six on the right-hand furnace tube, had melted through at the middle, the melted tin, lead, and zinc being found on the bottom of the shell in the form of shot.

An indication of the extent to which the furnace crowns had been overheated will be found in the fact that a lead strip laid across the right-hand tube at a distance of 14 feet from the front of the boiler, that is to say, 7 feet beyond the fire-bridge, was melted through. *There can be no doubt, therefore, that the furnace crown had been red-hot.*

Plate V. shows the arrangement of the dispersion pipe and the manner in which the water was showered on to the furnace crown. Plate X. shows the extent to which the furnace crowns were laid bare when the feed water was showered on to them. It also shows the position of the various fusible gauges, and of the lead strips, as well as the extent to which each lead strip was affected, and the furnace crown discoloured by overheating. Plate IX. shows the extent to which the zinc discs were melted, and Plate XI. the variations of pressure during the experiment.

SUPPLEMENTAL.

If it be supposed that the water on falling on the furnace crowns assumed a spheroidal condition so that a more rapid generation of steam would have taken place had the furnaces been less heated, it may be pointed out that the injection of the feed was continued from the first introduction of the shower until the furnaces were completely covered, so that the plates passed through all the gradations from red heat down to the temperature of the water in the boiler.

If it be asked: What would have been the result of making the experiment under a higher pressure of steam, say 80 lb. on the inch, it may be said that a furnace tube worked at such a pressure must have been strengthened with flanged seams, or other equivalent appliances. It could then have been dealt with under a pressure of 80 lb. with much greater safety than the experimental boiler at 30 lb., the furnace tubes of which were not strengthened with encircling rings. Had the experiments been conducted at a higher pressure, say at 50 lb. on the inch, it is doubtful whether the furnaces would have stood the effect of brisk, heavy fires for $23\frac{1}{2}$ minutes after the water had left the furnace crowns, and if not, the plates would not have been made so hot as they were and the test would not have been so complete, as the hotter the furnace crowns the greater the amount of steam which would be generated on the introduction of the feed.

As a record of facts is always useful, several little matters of detail have been described in the Report that would otherwise have been omitted. On reference to Experiment No. 2, it will be observed that with steam at a pressure of 40 lb. on the inch it took 4 minutes with the blow-out tap, $2\frac{1}{4}$ inches diameter, open full bore, to blow the water down to the level of the furnace crowns from a point 6 inches above them, and 4 minutes more to bring the water down to about 3 inches above the level of the firebars. The waste pipe in this case was about 90 feet long and had a bore of 3 inches. With a short waste pipe the discharge would have been more rapid. Ten minutes after the water had been brought down to the level of the furnace crowns the right hand tube collapsed. This information might have been of service to the steam user who lost his life by the collapse of a furnace crown at Hull on Friday, July 31st, 1874. In that case the blow-out tap had been opened and had stuck fast. The attendant was trying to shut it, but failing to do so collapse ensued, when both the attendant and the boiler owner were scalded to death. The information that in the experimental boiler the furnace crown collapsed under a pressure of 40 lb. on the inch 10 minutes after it was laid bare, may act as a useful warning to others in a somewhat similar position, while it should be remembered that with a higher pressure of steam the escape of water would be more rapid, and the collapse hastened.

SUMMARY.

The progress of the experiments has now been traced up from the beginning, and it has been shown how, step by step, the final result was arrived at of baring the furnace crowns under steam pressure, and keeping the fires briskly burning until the plates were red-hot, and then showering a bath of cold water upon them.

The experiments might have been extended further by way of

confirmation but for the objections that were raised on the score of danger. the boiler being, as already stated, within range of some public thoroughfares. Though the observers had confidence that no explosion would result from the injection of the cold water, yet, as previously explained, the experiments were somewhat difficult to manage, and not altogether free from risk. Brisk fires and red-hot furnace crowns under steam pressure were elements not easily controlled, and the fear was lest a collapse should occur unawares before the feed was injected and scatter the furnace mountings and brickwork, as has been the case in several explosions arising from collapse of the furnace tube; while further it was urged by some that the failure of one of the furnace tubes might extend to the rupture of the shell. and thus result in the destruction of the entire boiler, when the fragments would be blown in all directions. It would have been well if the boiler could have been set in the middle of a large field, so that if it exploded it would do so without risk to anyone but the experimenters.

The results obtained, however, showed that showering cold water on to the furnace crowns when red hot *did not lead to their rending by sudden contraction either transversely or longitudinally, nor did it lead to a violent generation of steam which the safety valves could not control and the shell could not resist.* On the injection of the feed when one of the safety valves was seated and the other open, the pressure rose in $1\frac{1}{4}$ minutes from 6 lb. to 12 lb., and when both safety valves were seated it rose in $\frac{3}{4}$ of a minute from 6 lb. to 27 lb., and then gradually fell. On the injection of the feed, when the safety valves were blowing, *no increase of pressure could be observed.* On the contrary it began to fall, and the hand of the pressure gauge to glide back. *There was no collapse; there was no rent, either in the furnace tubes or in the shell, and no movement of the boiler whatever.*

Such being the case, the question arises whether the experiments show that in the event of shortness of water it would be well to turn on the feed in every case?

The fact that when the feed was showered on to the red-hot furnace crowns with the safety valves blowing, as in Experiment No. 7, there was no rise of pressure, but on the contrary a fall, would seem to show that if the engine were running, so that any small amount of steam that might be generated by the injection of the feed would be carried off, the feed could be turned on with advantage, as it would tend to lower the pressure, restore the water level, and at the same time cool and re-invigorate the furnace plates. This would afford the attendant more time for drawing the fires and thus act in his protection.

On the other hand, however, the fact that when the feed was

showered on to the furnace crowns with one safety valve seated and the other open, as in Experiment No. 1, the pressure rose in 1¼ minutes from 6 lb. to 12 lb., and when the feed was showered on to the furnace crowns with the safety valves seated, as in Experiment No. 1A, and thus with the steam bottled up, the pressure rose in ¾ of a minute from 6 lb. to 27 lb., suggests the question whether if the engine were standing and the furnace crowns red-hot, the injection of the feed might not cause a rise of pressure of some 10 lb. or 20 lb., and whether this rise of pressure might not be sufficient to turn the scale and cause the furnace crowns to collapse, though it might not lead to the rending or displacement of the shell.

In reply to this it may be pointed out that in the experimental boiler, when the pressure was raised from 6 lb. to 12 lb. in one case and from 6 lb. to 27 lb. in another, the feed was not injected through a single "*ordinary*" dispersion pipe at one side of the boiler, and behind the firebridge, as in general practice, but through two specially contrived "*experimental*" dispersion pipes which injected the feed directly upon both furnace crowns just over the fire. The cases, therefore, are by no means parallel, while if the precaution were taken to ease the safety valves so as to allow them to blow freely and slightly reduce the pressure before turning on the feed, and if the feed dispersion pipe were made long enough to extend well back behind the firebridge, an arrangement which is recommended for general adoption, the probability of any increase of pressure on the injection of the feed would be very remote.

At the same time, however, it is thought that the experiments hardly allow of a positive opinion being formed on this point, and that further experiments would be necessary before this could be done. These would have been made had it been practicable. There were difficulties, however, in the way. Attempts to meet with another boiler in an isolated position in which the experiments could be safely prosecuted, even to the point of collapse, were advertised for and diligently sought, but without success, so that it was considered better to publish the report of what had been done, as a contribution to the general store of knowledge on this recondite subject, rather than to incur further delay.

The experiments, as far as they have been carried, lead to the conclusion that in the majority of cases turning on the feed, when delivered behind the fire bridge, would be the best thing to do. It would, as already stated, cool down the boiler, restore the water level, re-invigorate the plates of the furnace crowns, and be a safeguard to the attendant while he was drawing the fires. Still, it may be questioned if the experiments were of sufficient compass to meet every contingency that might arise in practice and to admit of a hard and fast rule being laid down that might be adopted absolutely under all circumstances without consideration or discretion. Many, on studying the results attained, might be disposed to take a bolder view, but as the question is one affecting the personal safety of boiler attendants, the difficulties attending its solution have been regarded in their most extreme aspect, and very possibly their importance has been exaggerated.

A Word to Boiler Attendants.

It is an extremely difficult and an extremely responsible task to give any recommendation with regard to the treatment of a boiler when short of water and working under steam pressure, that shall be applicable to every case under every variety of circumstance. A boiler attendant has no right to neglect his water supply and allow it to run short, nor has he a right to charge the fires without making sure that the furnace crowns are covered. Should he neglect these simple precautions, it is impossible to put matters right without some risk being run. A boiler with hot fires and with furnace crowns short of water is a dangerous instrument to deal with, and the attendant who has done the wrong must bear the risk.

The ordinary practice of drawing the fires is by no means unattended with danger. In the majority of cases it is difficult to tell how near the furnace is to the point of rending. All the time the attendant is drawing the fire he is standing directly in front of the furnace mouth, and thus in the line of danger. Should the furnace crown rend, a torrent of steam and hot water would be shot upon him. Fatal illustrations of the truth of this are not wanting.

At Clay Cross, near Chesterfield, on Thursday, January 14th, 1869, the attendant was in the act of drawing the fire from a Cornish boiler, overheated from shortness of water, when the furnace crown rent, and he was blown backwards to a distance of 25 yards, rake in hand, and killed on the spot.

A similar case occurred at Gorton, near Manchester, on Tuesday, September 15th, 1885. At half-past four o'clock in the morning, the attendant discovered that the water had disappeared from the gauge glass, and immediately began to draw the fires. While engaged in doing this the crown of the left furnace collapsed, and the attendant was so severely scalded that he died the same day.

Another case, though happily not fatal in its results, which occurred on Tuesday, October 23rd, 1877, may be referred to. At a quarter before two in the afternoon, when the boiler in question, which was one of a series, was in full work and the engine running, the fireman suddenly discovered on testing his glass water gauge, that he had mistaken an empty gauge glass for a full one. He had only just discovered his mistake and got as far as the front of the adjoining boiler, when the left-hand furnace crown came down, and a torrent of steam and hot water ensued. Fortunately, as he was out of the line of fire, he escaped injury. Had he commenced to draw the fires, there is no doubt he would have been severely scalded, as in the cases referred to above.

This will suffice to show that the ordinary practice of drawing the fires is sometimes attended with disastrous consequences.

After all, the best advice the M.S.U.A. can give to boiler attendants on this subject is :—*Do not let shortness of water occur.   Keep a sharp look-out on the water gauge.*

A Word to Boiler Owners.

If boiler owners would take the simple precaution of adopting low-water safety valves, there would be far fewer cases of shortness of water to deal with.   Low-water safety valves have now been well tried.   They have been in use at least a quarter of a century, and many thousands of them are now in work.   They are applied to all Lancashire or Cornish boilers made to the M.S.U.A. standard.

The feed should be introduced so that it would not be shot on to the furnaces, but delivered well behind the fire-bridge.

It would be of great service if a supplementary glass water gauge were provided and set low enough to show to what extent the furnace crowns were laid bare when the water was out of sight in the ordinary glasses.   This would be a guide to the boiler attendant as to whether it would be safe for him to draw his fires on the occurrence of shortness of water.

Conclusion.

These experiments clearly put to the rout the generally entertained opinion, that showering cold water on to red-hot furnace crowns would cause the "instantaneous disengagement of an immense volume of steam," which would act "like gunpowder," overpowering the safety valves, however efficient, tearing the outer shell of the boiler to pieces, and hurling the fragments to a considerable distance. Yet these opinions have been repeated again and again; the credence they have obtained has tended much to mystify the subject of steam boiler explosions, and, by leading astray from the true cause, to perpetuate the recurrence of these disasters. Many a poor fireman has been blamed for an explosion of which he was perfectly innocent.

It is trusted these experiments will be of public service, by helping to correct some of the mistaken views too generally entertained with regard to the cause of steam boiler explosions. It would have been well if they had been tried some fifty years ago, in the days when high-pressure steam was young. when the cause of steam boiler explosions was shrouded in mystery. and the easiest way out of the dilemma was to blame the stoker.

LAVINGTON E. FLETCHER,

Chief Engineer.

Manchester Steam Users' Association.
9, Mount Street, Albert Square, Manchester,
December 10th, 1889.

2500.
16.5.90.

APPENDIX.

APPENDIX.

SUPPLEMENTARY OBSERVATIONS,

TAKEN FROM ORDINARY MILL BOILERS, TO ASCERTAIN THE

DIFFERENCE OF TEMPERATURE

BETWEEN THE TOP AND THE BOTTOM OF THE WATER
WHEN GETTING UP STEAM.

As stated in the body of the Report (on page 18), it was thought that it might be well to supplement the observations with regard to the temperature of the water at the bottom and at the top when getting up steam in the experimental boiler, with similar observations on the temperature of the water when getting up steam in ordinary mill boilers, and with this view the following series of observations was made.

In order to make the series as extensive as possible, observations were made on the temperature in boilers both of the Lancashire and Galloway types, while the experiments were conducted with the boilers working under various conditions.

One of the Lancashire boilers experimented upon had no cross water-pipes in the internal flue tubes, and the other had four in each, while the Galloway boilers had thirty-three conical water-pipes and two side pockets in two cases, and thirty conical water-pipes and two pockets in the third case.

Both the Lancashire and Galloway boilers were set so that the gases immediately after leaving the flue tubes passed under the bottom, and, *lastly, along the sides*, except in the case of one Galloway boiler, in which the flames, immediately after leaving the oval flue-tube, passed along the sides, and, *lastly, under the bottom*. It is not easy to meet with a Lancashire boiler now-a-days set with the gases passing lastly under the bottom, at all events under the inspection of the M.S.U.A., or a series of observations would have been taken with a boiler set in that manner also.

Further, some observations were made with the boiler filled with cold water, as it would be in starting afresh after cleaning if all the boilers in the range were cold; others were made with the water slightly warmed, and others, again, with the boiler filled with water heated by passing through the economiser.

It is not thought necessary to give the entire number of observations in this Report, as it would render it very voluminous. Two complete tables, however, are given, one, of the observations taken from a Lancashire boiler (page 54), and the other, from a Galloway boiler (page 55), in order to show the way in which the record was kept. The principal points of all the observations are given in a condensed form in the tables below.

Mode of Conducting the Experiments.

For taking the observations two test taps were fixed to the front end plate, as in the experimental boiler, for drawing off the water, one of these being fixed about 3 inches above the level of the furnace crowns and the other about 8 inches above the bottom of the shell. Each tap was fitted with an internal pipe, having a bore of $\frac{3}{4}$ inch, and carried into the boiler for a length of 3 feet, so as not to draw the water off close to the front end.

In taking the temperature of the water a new thermometer made and guaranteed by Casartelli was used. The bulb was held directly in the stream of water issuing from the test tap.

As the temperature of the water issuing from the test taps was taken at atmospheric pressure, it could not under any circumstances exceed 212°, whatever might be the temperature of the water inside the boiler. The temperatures, therefore, of the top of the water, when given in the Table as above 212°, have been arrived at by calculation from the pressure indicated by the steam gauge. See Table in D. K. Clark's Mechanical Engineers' Manual, based on the investigations of Regnault. As, however, the pressure of steam is no indication of the temperature of the water at the bottom of the boiler, the observation of the temperature of the water at the bottom of the boiler could not be carried above 212°, and therefore at that point the experiments ceased.

In each case the firemen were instructed to fire gently and get up steam gradually, just as if no observations were being taken. The dampers were raised sufficiently to clear away the smoke freely and allow the fires to burn slowly until the pressure of steam in the boiler was sufficiently high to allow of the stop valve being opened and the boiler put in connection with the others at work in the range, when the dampers were further opened and a full share of draught given.

Observations were taken every five minutes of the temperature of the water at the bottom as well as at the top, and also of the pressure of steam as soon as it arose.

LANCASHIRE Boiler A.

Length, 32 feet; diameter of shell, 8 feet; diameter of furnaces, 3 feet 2 inches; length of firegrate, 6 feet 6 inches. Four cross water-pipes in each internal flue tube.

Boiler set so that the flames immediately after leaving the internal flue tubes passed under the bottom of the shell, and *lastly along the sides.*

Boiler filled with cold water, as it would be in starting afresh after cleaning if all the boilers in the range were cold.

No. 1. *

Length of time from Lighting Fires.		Steam Pressure.	Temperature at the Top.	Temperature at the Bottom.	Difference.
Hrs.	Mins.				
0	0	.. ..	58°	58°	0°
1	45	.. ..	212°	72°	140°
†2	20	75 lb.	320°	84°	236°
3	20	62 lb.	309°	133°	176°

* NOTE.—This experiment was not completed when the time for stopping the mill arrived, and therefore had to be cut short before a temperature of 212° at the bottom of the boiler was reached.

† At this point the stop valve was opened and the boiler put in connection with the others at work in the range : at the same time the dampers were opened wide.

Boiler filled with cold water the day previous, and slightly warmed up by contiguity to the other boilers working alongside.

No. 2.   No. 2A. ‡

Length of time from Lighting Fires.	Steam Pressure.	Temperature at Top.	Temperature at Bottom.	Difference.	Length of time from Lighting Fires.	Steam Pressure	Temperature at Top.	Temperature at Bottom.	Difference.
Hrs. Mins.					Hrs. Mins.				
0 0	..	103°	99°	4°	0 0	..	84°	76°	8°
1 20	..	212°	106°	106°	1 55	..	212°	88°	124°
†2 0	72 lb.	318°	114°	204°	†3 25	79 lb.	323°	105°	218°
3 25	64 lb.	311°	212°	99°	6 5	81 lb.	325°	212°	113°

‡ NOTE.—This experiment was protracted, owing to the dampers having to be closed for one hour during the stoppage of the mill at dinner time.

† At this point the stop valve was opened and the boiler put in connection with the others at work in the range : at the same time the damper was opened wide.

Boiler filled with water heated by passing through the Economiser.

No. 3.

Length of time from Lighting Fires.		Steam Pressure.	Temperature at Top.	Temperature at Bottom.	Difference.
Hrs.	Mins.				
0	0	.. ..	198°	180°	18°
0	30	.. ..	212°	182°	30°
†1	10	72 lb.	318°	189°	129°
1	52	71 lb.	317°	212°	105°

† At this point the stop valve was opened and the boiler put in connection with the others at work in the range : at the same time the damper was opened wide.

LANCASHIRE Boiler B.

Length, 28 feet; diameter of shell, 7 feet; diameter of furnaces, 2 feet 7½ inches; length of fire grate, 6 feet. No cross water-pipes in flue tubes.

Boiler set so that the flames immediately after leaving the internal flue tubes passed under the bottom of the shell, and *lastly along the sides.*

Boiler filled with cold water, as it would be in starting afresh after cleaning if all the boilers in the range were cold.

No. 4.

Length of time from Lighting Fires.		Steam Pressure.	Temperature at Top.	Temperature at Bottom.	Difference.
Hrs.	Mins.				
0	0	.. ..	58°	57°	1°
2	20	.. ..	212°	96°	116°
†3	45	52 lb.	300°	132°	168°
4	20	51 lb.	299°	212°	87°

† At this point the stop valve was opened and the boiler put in connection with the others at work in the range, and at the same time the damper was opened wide.

GALLOWAY Boiler A.

Length, 30 feet; diameter of shell, 7 feet; diameter of furnaces, 2 feet 9 inches; length of fire grate, 6 feet. Thirty-three conical water-pipes and two side pockets in the oval flue tube.

Boiler set so that the flames immediately after leaving the internal flue tubes passed under the bottom of the shell, *and lastly along the sides.*

Boiler filled with cold water, as it would be in starting afresh if all the boilers in the range were cold.

No. 5.

Length of time from Lighting Fires.		Steam Pressure.	Temperature at Top.	Temperature at Bottom.	Difference.
Hrs.	Mins.				
0	0	.. ..	67°	64°	3°
2	5	.. ..	212°	78°	134°
†2	55	72 lb.	316°	87°	231°
4	5	63 lb.	310°	212°	98°

† At this point the stop valve was opened and the boiler put in connection with the others at work in the range : at the same time the damper was opened wide.

Boiler filled with water heated by passing through the economiser.

No. 6.

Length of Time from Lighting Fires.		Steam Pressure.	Temperature at Top.	Temperature at Bottom.	Difference.
Hrs.	Mins.				
0	0	.. ..	150°	150°	6°
0	55	.. ..	212°	155°	57°
†1	30	71 lb.	317°	162°	155°
2	25	72 lb.	318°	212°	106°

† At this point the stop valve was opened and the boiler put in connection with the others at work in the range : at the same time the damper was opened wide.

GALLOWAY Boiler B.

Length, 30 feet; diameter of the shell, 7 feet; diameter of furnaces, 2 feet 9 inches; length of fire grate, 6 feet. Thirty-three conical water-pipes and two side pockets in the oval flue tube.

Boiler set so that the flames immediately after leaving the oval flue tube passed under the bottom of the shell, and *lastly along the sides.*

Boiler filled with cold water, as it would be in starting afresh if all the boilers in the range were cold.

No. 7.

Length of time from Lighting Fires.		Steam Pressure.	Temperature at Top.	Temperature at Bottom.	Difference.
Hrs.	Mins.				
0	0	.. ..	49°	46°	3°
2	30	.. ..	212°	71°	141°
†3	20	80 lb.	324°	94°	230°
4	10	76 lb.	321°	212°	109°

† At this point the stop valve was opened and the boiler put in connection with the others at work in the range : at the same time the damper was opened wide.

Boiler filled with water heated by passing through the economiser.

No. 8.

Length of time from Lighting Fires.		Steam Pressure.	Temperature at Top.	Temperature at Bottom.	Difference.
Hrs.	Mins.				
0	0	.. ..	187°	147°	40°
0	30	.. ..	212°	148°	64°
†2	0	80 lb.	324°	162°	162°
2	37	81 lb.	325°	212°	113°

† At this point the stop valve was opened and the boiler put in connection with the others at work in the range : at the same time the damper was opened wide.

GALLOWAY Boiler C.

Length, 28 feet ; diameter of shell, 7 feet ; diameter of furnaces, 2 feet 9 inches ; length of fire grate, 4 feet 8 inches. Thirty conical water-pipes and two side pockets in the oval flue tube.

Boiler set so that the flames immediately after leaving the oval flue tube passed along the sides of the shell, and *lastly under the bottom.*

Boiler filled with cold water, as it would be in starting afresh if all the boilers in the range were cold.

No. 9.

Length of time from Lighting Fires.		Steam Pressure.	Temperature at Top.	Temperature at Bottom.	Difference.
Hrs.	Mins.				
0	0		61°	61°	0°
1	50	.. ..	212°	70°	142°
†3	0	53 lb.	301°	76°	225°
4	35	59 lb.	307°	212°	95°

† At this point the stop valve was opened and the boiler put in connection with the others at work in the range : at the same time the dampers were opened wide.

It may be of convenience if the results of the experiments are grouped together, as follows :—

WITH THE TEMPERATURE OF THE WATER AT 212° AT THE TOP.

Boiler filled with Cold Water.

Experiment No. 1. Lancashire Boiler A	..	Top, 212°	..	Bottom, 72°	..	Difference,	140°
" No. 4. Lancashire Boiler B	..	" 212°	..	" 96°	..	"	116°
" No. 5. Galloway Boiler A	....	" 212°	..	" 78°	..	"	134°
" No. 7. Galloway Boiler B	....	" 212°	..	" 71°	..	"	141°
" No. 9. Galloway Boiler C	....	" 212°	..	" 70°	..	"	142°

Mean.... 134°

Boiler filled with Tepid Water.

Experiment No. 2. Lancashire Boiler A .. Top, 212° .. Bottom, 106° .. Difference, 106°
" No. 2A. Lancashire Boiler A.. " 212° .. " 88° .. " 124°

Mean.... 115°

Boiler filled with Hot Water.

Experiment No. 3. Lancashire Boiler A.... Top, 212° .. Bottom, 182° .. Difference, 30°
" No. 6. Galloway Boiler A .... " 212° .. " 155° .. " 57°
" No. 8. Galloway Boiler B .... " 212° .. " 148° .. " 64°

Mean.... 50°

WHEN THE STOP VALVE WAS OPENED, AND THE BOILER PUT IN CONNECTION WITH THE OTHERS AT WORK IN THE RANGE.

Boiler filled with Cold Water.

Experiment No. 1. Lancashire Boiler A.... Top, 320° .. Bottom, 84° .. Difference, 236°
" No. 4. Lancashire Boiler B .. " 300° .. " 132° .. " 168°
" No. 5. Galloway Boiler A .... " 318° .. " 87° .. " 231°
" No. 7. Galloway Boiler B .... " 324° .. " 94° .. " 230°
" No. 9. Galloway Boiler C .... " 301° .. " 76° .. " 225°

Mean.... 218°

Boiler filled with Tepid Water.

Experiment No. 2. Lancashire Boiler A .. Top, 318° .. Bottom, 114° .. Difference, 204°
" No. 2A. Lancashire Boiler A.. " 323° .. " 105° .. " 218°

Mean.... 211°

Boiler filled with Hot Water.

Experiment No. 3. Lancashire Boiler A .. Top, 318° .. Bottom, 189° .. Difference, 129°
" No. 6. Galloway Boiler A.... " 317° .. " 162° .. " 155°
" No. 8. Galloway Boiler B.... " 324° .. " 162° .. " 162°

Mean.... 148°

When the water at the bottom of the boiler was at a temperature of 212° only, steam at the top of the boiler had risen in three cases to above 70 lb. pressure, and in two cases to above 80 lb. pressure, while the greatest difference in temperature observed was as high as 236°.

DEDUCTIONS.

It would not be fair to draw a *minute* comparison between the results obtained from the different boilers, unless the temperatures of the water at the commencement of the experiments, the strength of the draught, the intensity of the fire, and all the conditions under which the boilers were worked were the same in every particular, but the following *broad* deductions may it is thought be drawn :—

Firstly, that in ordinary mill boilers the temperature, when getting up steam, is much higher at the top of the water than at the bottom.

Secondly, that this inequality is practically the same, whether in a Lancashire boiler with four cross water pipes in each flue tube, or in a Lancashire boiler without any cross water pipes at all, or in a Galloway boiler with thirty-three conical water pipes and two pockets, or with thirty conical water pipes and two pockets.

Thirdly, that it appears that water pipes are not as efficient in promoting circulation of water throughout the boiler as the public has generally supposed.

The M.S.U.A. has been very cautious in recommending the adoption of water pipes, and these experiments would appear to justify the caution it has exercised.

Precautions to be taken to Prevent Straining.

Seeing that the difference of temperature between the top and the bottom of the water when getting up steam tends more or less to strain the boiler, it is desirable to reduce that difference as much as possible, and several plans have been proposed with that object.

One plan is to apply a screw or other similar appliance for promoting the circulation of the water inside the boiler mechanically, and thus to compel the hot to mix with the cold, though such an arrangement has not come into general use.

Another plan for promoting the circulation of the water mechanically, which has been adopted in marine boilers—in which the difficulty arising from the inequality of the temperature at the top of the water and the bottom is severely felt—is to fix a description of injector inside the boiler. This injector has to be fed with steam from another boiler, either from one in the range or an auxiliary one. This plan has been attended with success.

No mechanical arrangements, however, for promoting the circulation of the water have been generally applied to mill boilers, and much can be done to reduce straining when getting up steam simply by careful treatment of the boiler.

On referring to the Tables it will be seen that the inequality between the temperature at the top and at the bottom of the water when getting up steam was considerably reduced by filling up the boiler with hot water pumped in through the economiser. It might, therefore, be well to adopt this plan whenever it is practicable to do so.

It will also be seen that advantage was gained where there were other boilers working alongside, by allowing the water to stand in the boiler a day or so before lighting the fires, so that it might be slightly warmed up by contiguity to the boilers in work. This plan, though not so efficacious as the preceding one, might be adopted with advantage where hot water for filling up purposes cannot be had.

Further, it is advisable to get up steam with slow fires, so as to heat the boilers up gradually, otherwise the furnace tubes become considerably hogged, and straining takes place at the furnace mouth and at the bottom rivets of the gusset stays in the front end plate. In illustration of this, it may be stated that in every experiment in which the boiler was filled up with cold water to start with, slight leakages commenced at the attachment of the furnaces to the front end plate at about the middle of the experiment, but took up before it was finished. Where practicable the fires should be lighted over night, so that the boiler may be gradually warmed up for some ten or twelve hours before opening the stop valve and putting the boiler in connection with the others at work in the range.

It may be added that it might be of advantage on some occasions when getting up steam to open the blow-out tap for a short time, so as to lower the water a few inches, and thus to blow out the cold water from the bottom of the boiler and draw the hot water down from the top.

Where the simple precautions recommended above are adopted in boilers of the ordinary Lancashire or Galloway type, and the boilers are well made, little practical difficulty is experienced.

LAVINGTON E. FLETCHER,

Chief Engineer.

Manchester Steam Users' Association,
9, Mount Street, Albert Square, Manchester,
June 17th, 1890.

LANCASHIRE Boiler B.

Length 28 feet; diameter of shell 7 feet; diameter of furnace 2 feet 7¼ inches; length of fire grate 6 feet. No cross water pipes in flue tubes.

Boiler set so that the flames, immediately after leaving the internal flue tubes, passed under the bottom of the shell, and *lastly along the sides.*

No. 4.

Fires lighted at 12-30 p.m.

Time.	Steam Press-ure.	TEMPERATURE.			Time.	Steam Press-ure.	TEMPERATURE.		
		Top.	Bottom.	Difference.			Top.	Bottom.	Difference.
	lbs.					lbs.			
12 30	0	58°	57°	1°	2 45	0	202°	94°	108°
12 35	0	58°	57°	1°	2 50	0	212°	96°	116°
12 40	0	59°	57°	2°	2 55	0	212°	98°	114°
12 45	0	64°	57°	7°	3 0	2	220°	100°	120°
12 50	0	68°	57°	11°	3 5	5	228°	101°	127°
12 55	0	72°	58°	14°	3 10	8	236°	103°	133°
1 0	0	76°	58°	18°	3 15	12	244°	106°	138°
1 5	0	81°	60°	21°	3 20	15	250°	108°	142°
1 10	0	84°	60°	24°	3 25	19	258°	111°	147°
1 15	0	89°	61°	28°	3 30	21	261°	114°	147°
1 20	0	94°	62°	32°	3 35	23	264°	117°	147°
1 25	0	98	63°	35°	3 40	26	269°	119°	150°
1 30	0	102°	64°	38°	3 45	29	273°	121°	152°
1 35	0	110°	66°	44°	3 50	33	278°	122°	156°
1 40	0	121°	68°	53°	3 55	36	282°	124°	158°
1 45	0	128°	70°	58°	4 0	39	286°	127°	159°
1 50	0	134°	72°	62°	4 5	42	289°	129°	160°
1 55	0	140°	74°	66°	4 10	46	294°	130°	164°
2 0	0	150°	76°	74°	†4 15	52	300°	132°	168°
2 5	0	158°	78°	80°	4 20	50	298°	134°	164°
2 10	0	164°	80°	84°	4 25	52	300°	*136° to 138°	164° to 162°
2 15	0	170°	82°	88°	4 30	52	300°	*142° to 144°	158° to 156°
2 20	0	176°	84°	92°	4 35	52	300°	*145° to 150°	155° to 150°
2 25	0	180°	86°	94°	4 40	52	300°	*158° to 162°	142° to 138°
2 30	0	184°	88°	96°	4 45	52	300°	*200° to 206°	100° to 94°
2 35	0	190°	90°	100°	4 50	51	299°	212°	87°
2 40	0	196°	91°	105°					

† At this point the stop valve was opened and the boiler connected with the others at work in the range; at the same time the dampers were opened wide.

* At these points the temperature fluctuated between the limits given, thus showing that the water was in rapid motion.

www.ingramcontent.com/pod-product-compliance
Lightning Source LLC
Chambersburg PA
CBHW021639270326
41931CB00008B/1086